THE OTHER SIDE

HOW SOVIETS AND AMERICANS
PERCEIVE EACH OTHER

THE OTHER SIDE

HOW SOVIETS AND AMERICANS
PERCEIVE EACH OTHER

Robert English and Jonathan J. Halperin

From the Series **Beyond the Kremlin**
A Publication of the Committee for National Security

Transaction Publishers
New Brunswick (U.S.A.) and London (U.K.)

Fourth Printing, 1990

Copyright © 1987 by the Committee for National Security.

Printed in the United States of America.

91   90   5   4

Library of Congress Cataloging-in-Publication Data

The Other Side.

    Bibliography: p.
    Includes index.
    1. United States — Foreign opinion, Russian.   2. Soviet
Union — Foreign opinion, American.   3. Public opinion —
United States.   4. Public opinion — Soviet Union.
I. Halperin, Jonathan J., 1958-
E183.8.S65O84 1987   327.73047   86-30805
ISBN 0-88738-687-3 (pbk.)

Designed by Meadows & Wiser, Washington, D.C.

Cover illustration by Matt Mahurin.

Composed in Century Expanded and Franklin Gothic by General Typographers, Inc., Washington, D.C.

Printed by Edwards Brothers, Inc., Ann Arbor, Michigan.

COMMITTEE FOR NATIONAL SECURITY

A national organization with headquarters in Washington, DC, the Committee for National Security (CNS) informs Americans about national security and arms control issues and encourages active citizen participation in the ongoing debate over U.S. military and foreign policy. The Committee was founded in 1980 and currently has 11 full-time professional staff. The membership of the Committee is composed of prominent citizens concerned about our nation's drift toward excessive reliance on military power to resolve complex foreign policy problems. The Committee is a nonprofit and tax-exempt organization located at 1601 Connecticut Avenue, NW, Suite 301, Washington, DC 20009; (202) 745-2450.

Project Manager and Series Editor
Jonathan J. Halperin

Senior Soviet Analyst and Principal Contributor
Robert D. English

Consultant
Sarah deKay

Research
Robert English, Jonathan J. Halperin, James M. Hochman, Anne Hoving, Christine Janezick, Julia Rochez

Production
Carl Manello, Mark Niedergang, Lynn Whittemore

Correspondence, Marketing, and Permissions
Susan Dargusch, Barbara Gertel, Christine Janezick, Kathy Ladun, Aleza Martin, Cindy Scharf

Project Development
Anne H. Cahn, Jo L. Husbands

Copy Editor
Martha S. Cooley

SOVIET RESOURCE PANEL

Robert Donaldson, President, Fairleigh Dickinson University; *Herbert Ellison*, Jackson School of International Relations, University of Washington; *Raymond Garthoff*, Brookings Institution; *Marshall Goldman*, Associate Director, Russian Research Center, Harvard University; *Nancy Ignatius*, Board Member, Committee for National Security; *Lawrence Kaagan*, Senior Vice President, Daniel Yankelovich Group; *Gail Lapidus*, Professor of Political Science, University of California, Berkeley, and Chair, Berkeley-Stanford Program on Soviet International Behavior; *Jonathan Sanders*, Assistant Director, W. Averell Harriman Institute for Advanced Study of the Soviet Union; *Robert Schmidt*, Chairman, American Committee on East-West Accord; *Colette Shulman*, Researcher and Consultant on Soviet Affairs; *Dimitri Simes*, Senior Associate, Carnegie Endowment for International Peace.

ACKNOWLEDGMENTS

In preparing this book of selected readings we have called on the assistance of many people: scholars, educators, journalists, government officials, and historians. In some cases we have queried people repeatedly in our search for a fact, a date, or a quotation. Others we have called on only once, seeking help on an obscure or difficult question. If this book is enriching to our readers, that is in large part due to the good-natured and patient advice offered by dozens of people across the country. We are especially grateful for the help provided by Jonathan Sanders, Ellen Mickiewicz, Sophie Silberberg and the staff at the Fund for Free Expression, Robert C. Tucker, Tom Graham, Dorothy Fall, and Dorothy Atkinson. We also gratefully acknowledge the generous support of the following funders: Anne Bartley, Allen Hilles Fund, Margaret V. H. Hubbard, W. Alton Jones Foundation, New Land Foundation, Ploughshares Fund, Anne Roberts, Rockefeller Family Fund, Samuel Rubin Foundation, and an anonymous donor.

The following people read all or parts of the draft manuscript: Susan Alexander, Anne Cahn, Richard Ellison, Raymond Garthoff, Marshall Goldman, Mark Hainline, Mary Hey, Jo Husbands, Nancy Ignatius, Lawrence Kaagan, Carl Maeirick, Suzanna O'Donnell, Peter Reddaway, Cindy Scharf, Colette Shulman, Robert Schmidt, Janet Vaillant, Lynn Wildman, and Adam Yarmolinsky. Their cautions, criticisms, and suggestions were invaluable, steering us clear of factual errors and helping us focus on specific educational goals. Despite the good advice we received, errors may remain; they are solely the fault of the authors.

The preparation of this manuscript would not have been possible without the permissions CNS was granted to reprint copyrighted textual and graphic materials, and we are especially grateful to those who granted such permission without charge. The resources and staff of the Library of Congress were also essential to our research. For consistent good humor and faith we owe a debt of gratitude to all our colleagues at the Committee for National Security: from our patient and determined director to our dedicated volunteers.

JJH and RDE
Washington, DC, 1986

BEYOND THE KREMLIN

SERIES INTRODUCTION

We have been on a blind date with the Soviet Union for decades. Although skeptical about our compatibility, we have been unable, often unwilling, to end the relationship. We fear what might happen.

We have tried working things out. We have challenged each other, "eyeball to eyeball," in Cuba and Berlin. We have signed documents, held meetings, and consulted with friends about what to do. We have tried to cooperate and build on common interests. But still we remain unsure, ambivalent, worried about how to handle this troubled relationship. What should we do? Can we learn to live with the Soviet Union? Can we afford not to?

Even to begin tackling these questions, we need to know more about the Union of Soviet Socialist Republics, and that is the goal of this series: to enable Americans to assess more accurately the Soviet Union — its policies, goals, people, culture, and problems. There are, however, numerous obstacles. Language is a problem. Travel is restricted. The Soviets make it difficult for journalists and scholars to prepare books and articles accurately portraying the state of affairs in their country. This penchant for secrecy and distortion is part of the dark, menacing side of the Soviet Union: its controlled press, its limited freedoms, its lack of what our Declaration of Independence calls "unalienable rights."

In addition, educating ourselves about the Soviet Union is difficult because we are now adversaries. We treat each other as such, competing for power, access to resources, and influence around the globe — from Poland to Nicaragua and the Philippines. Our leaders point at each other, posturing for their audiences. Being enemies in the nuclear age carries enormous risks; the stakes could not get much higher. Fears are heightened, time for reflection and judgment is shortened, and reasoned discourse can be (and often is) replaced by anxious rhetoric. Ideological differences present yet another obstacle. We believe in and live by different sets of principles. Communism and democracy represent alternative ways of organizing society, and they embody powerfully contrasting views about the role of individuals in politics and society.

One of the greatest strengths of democratic nations is that they preserve for their citizens the right to know and learn and talk about systems of government and ideologies that differ from their own. By exercising this right, we can help ourselves and our nation. We need to know more about the Soviet Union, a country that is so important but with which we have had such a stormy relationship. There are expansive political, even philosophical, questions crying out for our attention. What really makes the Soviets tick? What does the invasion of Afghanistan mean? Is Gorbachev really going to be different? Can religion survive in a Communist state? And there are small, even simple, questions too — but questions we also need to address before we can know what the Soviet Union is all about. What do the people eat? What do they read, and do for pleasure, and wear? Do they watch TV? What are Soviet schools like? Do children go to summer camp? What is the divorce rate? Do mothers work?

The books in this series are organized topically and address both broad political questions and precise factual ones. Each book can be read by itself or in conjunction with other parts of the series. A list of the other books planned for the *Beyond the Kremlin* series is in the Reader's Guide.

As you begin to probe the complexity of the Soviet Union by thinking about the readings in *Beyond the Kremlin,* you will almost certainly imagine more questions than we have been able to ask or answer. The Reader's Guide, which includes an annotated reading list, suggests some ways in which you might pursue your questions. The Reader's Guide offers suggestions on how to organize discussion groups, how to lead discussions, and some questions to consider. It also briefly describes other educational activities that might complement or flow from participation in a discussion group. Although a discussion group is not essential to enjoying and benefiting from the material, its give-and-take may be stimulating and helpful in trying to understand the U.S.S.R.

The relationship in which we are enmeshed with the Soviet Union is complex, confusing, and sometimes frightening. It is, however, a relationship, and the Soviet Union is a nation we need to know more about. The cost of remaining uninformed is high. By its very nature, a blind date does not last forever.

CONTENTS

INTRODUCTION

Without ever having been to the Soviet Union, most of us can nonetheless easily create mental snapshots of this land and its people: onion-topped buildings; people in dark, bulky winter coats standing in line; aging leaders in a row atop the Kremlin wall.

What are the sources of these images? Like all images, they result from the vast array of information gathered over time by our senses. For many of us, reading — an extension of seeing — has powerfully informed our vision of the Soviet Union. But it is through all our senses that we experience our world, and the more of our sensing ability we can bring to bear on any particular subject, the better able we are to understand it. From the raw information our senses collect, we generate meanings for what is happening around us.

As we grow, constantly learning and interpreting, we distinguish among various types of information. We develop a mental hierarchy: certain sights, tastes, sounds, or smells become so familiar that we take them for granted, reserving our energies instead to grapple with new, unfamiliar sensations and situations. The taste of milk, for instance, is something we recognize so quickly that we do not so much interpret it as simply accept it for what it is. We come to know the taste simply as an aspect of reality. Similarly, we know, as seemingly immutable facts, that the sky is blue and the earth is round. By necessity we distinguish such facts, with which we need not concern ourselves, from other matters that demand critical interpretation.

Through this process of sorting, we develop a feel for those things which are reasonably certain as distinct from those which remain unclear, confusing, and in flux. When something that once seemed certain suddenly once again requires interpretation, we are forced to pause — caught short, asked to rethink what a moment ago we took for granted.

These moments often come about unexpectedly. For example, going

How do we come to know what we know about another nation?

11

> **"Facts do not speak for themselves, but are given meaning by each interpreter from his own . . . point of view. The conclusion that follows from facts depends on the interpretation that is given to the facts."**
> Walter S. Jones, Wayne State University

back as an adult to a childhood home and showing a friend that "big tree in the yard" or the "long dark hall" can be a humbling experience: the tree may not appear so large, the hall so long. When this happens — when present reality sharply contradicts deeply held perceptions — we feel uneasy, made aware that how we see things may be very closely related to who we are.

As can happen when we return to childhood homes only to find them transformed, our shared national perceptions can be similarly jolted. In foreign affairs one of the starkest examples of such a profound change in attitudes is our relationship with China. After decades of referring to this nation as "Red China" and openly using hostile and insulting language (the "Yellow Peril"), we have recently come to accept this nation and its people as regular members of the international community. No doubt a host of factors contributed to this change in our perceptions. It bears remembering, however, that before the change took place, our prior perceptions were so firmly held that most of us viewed normal relations as virtually impossible.

The relationship of China and the U.S. is not, however, a model for other international relationships, and certainly not for our relationship with the Soviet Union. Each such relationship has its unique history, complexities, and subtleties. Ours with the Soviet Union is particularly complex. Soviet and American perceptions spring from vastly different historical, cultural, and personal experiences. But our perceptions of each other are no less real for this lack of common experience. Because few of us are likely to travel to the Soviet Union and experience firsthand the bustle of a Ukrainian peasant market, feel the pride of a young child reciting a Pushkin poem from memory, or sense the cool, damp air that surrounds visitors to Lenin's tomb, we must rely on others' experiences as the basis of our perceptions.

The following four sections of this book focus on four of the major forces that influence perceptions. The first section illustrates some of the ways in which Soviet and American perceptions have influenced and been influenced by history. The effects of the news media are the subject of section two. Sections three and four deal with books and movies, respectively, and how each contributes to Soviet and American perceptions.

POLITICAL HISTORY

WHO, WHAT, WHEN, AND WHERE

No international relationship is as critical to the security of the entire world as that of the U.S. and the U.S.S.R. With both nations possessing the means to destroy civilization, a stable relationship is in everyone's best interest.

Despite this need, for nearly 70 years the history of U.S.-Soviet relations has been marked by alternating periods of cooperation and confrontation. We have swung like a pendulum from being allies to being adversaries, from peace to the brink of war. And as U.S.-Soviet relations have fluctuated, so too have the images each side holds of the other. From understanding and friendship to mistrust and hatred, the history of U.S.-Soviet mutual perceptions is even more erratic than the actual relations of the two countries.

As these actual relations have improved or soured, the perceptions each side has of the other have naturally shifted. But perceptions themselves have also caused shifts in our relations. When proceeding from knowledge and understanding, U.S.-Soviet relations have been fairly stable. When enveloped in misconceptions and unrealistic expectations, these relations have fluctuated precariously. Thus, perceptions have been and remain both an effect and a cause of shifts in U.S.-Soviet relations. History has shown us that images are as important as realities in international relations.

But what can account for the drastic shifts in our perceptions of the Soviets, and in theirs of us? From the "Red scares" of the 1920s to the "fellow travelers" of the 1930s, from spies and "wreckers" under Stalin's terror to allies united against Hitler, from McCarthyism to "peaceful coexistence" and from cold war to detente — what is behind these volatile swings?

Some of these swings can be traced to the many differences between U.S. and Soviet society and culture. American society has a long tradi-

"We must appreciate the images of the past before we can fully comprehend our current dilemma."

▌ 15

1867

U.S. purchases Alaska from Russia

1905

Revolution; Tsar relinquishes some authority; Duma (legislature) formed

1917

February: Russian Revolution; Tsar abdicates; provisional government headed by Kerensky

tion of democracy and freedom; Soviet (and before that, Russian) society has always been autocratic and authoritarian. While we cherish diversity and individual liberties, Soviets value order and conformity. Where we see variety and opportunity, Soviets see chaos and insecurity. Even many Soviets who criticize the deadening repression of communism are suspicious of the "disorder" and "decadence" of Western democracy. And although many Americans lament the problems of unemployment or irresponsibility, few of us would trade them for the Soviet version of cradle-to-grave social services and Communist morality.

American and Soviet historical experiences are also radically different. Whereas the U.S. encountered relatively little resistance in expanding to cover most of the continent, the original Russian nation fought repeatedly for its survival in a much longer struggle to secure the current borders of the Soviet Union. Americans have rarely known the threat of foreign attackers on our soil; Russians have endured invasions from the Tatars, Swedes, Poles, French, Germans, and others (see "Invasions and Occupations" on this page). These historical experiences remain powerful forces shaping our relations today. The Soviets do not comprehend our impulsive and open nature, and we have difficulty understanding their obsession with the sanctity of borders and buffer zones.

Finally, there are the differences in the American and Russian national personality. As Americans we are proud of our standing as the world's foremost political and economic power, and of our leadership in the community of nations. Russian and Soviet history is a much longer story of backwardness and isolation. Efforts by such reformers as Peter the Great (1682–1725) to force Russia to adopt modern technology and Western customs have been the exception, not the rule. Despite the Soviet Union's modern military might, its persistent backwardness in other aspects of technology and economic development perpetuates the gap between East and West. Despite its great effect on world affairs, the Soviet Union remains isolated and surrounded by hostile neighbors.

Accepting the historical differences between our two societies and cultures is essential to understanding the perceptions that now dominate U.S. and Soviet thinking. We must appreciate the images of the past before we can fully comprehend our current dilemma.

When the Bolsheviks (Communists) seized power in Russia on November 7, 1917, the entire world was shocked. As Russia pulled out of World War I, Bolshevik leader V. I. Lenin (born Vladimir Ilyich Ulyanov)

INVASIONS AND OCCUPATIONS OF RUSSIA AND THE SOVIET UNION

Invader	Date
Tatars (Mongols)	1223–1480
Teutonic Knights	1280s
Poland and Sweden	1600s
Sweden	1708–1709
France (Napoleon)	1812
Germany (World War I)	1914–1918
England, France, U.S., Italy, Canada, Japan et al.	1918–1922
Poland	1920–1921
Germany (World War II)	1941–1944

1917

November: Bolshevik Revolution overthrows provisional government

1918

March: Treaty of Brest-Litovsk with Germany; Russia leaves WWI

1918–1921

Civil War; Bolsheviks ("Reds") eventually defeat counter-revolutionaries ("Whites"); Allied intervention

appealed to the masses on both sides of the trenches to rise up and cast off their capitalist-imperialist rulers. In addition to this, the atheism and perceived immorality of the new Soviet regime were particularly repugnant to American sensibilities. Soviet pronouncements about the inevitability of worldwide Communist revolution, as well as the nation's stated intention to promote it, contributed to a "Red scare" that swept the U.S. in 1919 and 1920. Thousands of suspected Bolshevik agents or sympathizers were arrested, and hundreds were deported. Fear, ignorance, and threatening Soviet pronouncements combined to produce distorted images of the new Soviet Union, views that sometimes had very little to do with reality.

The following excerpts from a speech by Montana Senator Henry L. Myers illustrate anti-Soviet propaganda during this period. The "bureau of free love" he describes never existed; the cited decree is a fake.

"Each of the great powers fears the power, the ideas, the social system of the other."

During the allied intervention in 1918-1920, these Canadian and American soldiers landed in the Soviet Union.

Bettman Archive.

1921
"New Economic Policy" permits some private enterprise

1921–1922
Widespread famine

1924
January: Lenin dies

Congressional Record, April 28, 1920, as quoted in Peter Filene, *American Views of Soviet Russia* (Homewood, IL: Dorsey Press, 1968), pp. 38–40.

What do we perceive today as most threatening about the U.S.S.R. — its Communist ideology or military power?

A decree issued by the Soviet of the city of Vladimir follows:

Any girl having reached her eighteenth year and not having married is obliged, subject to the most severe penalty, to register at the bureau of free love of the commissariat of surveillance.

Having registered at the bureau of free love, she has the right to choose from among the men between the ages of 19 and 50 a cohabitant husband. . . .

The right to choose from a number of girls who have reached their eighteenth year is also given to men.

The opportunity to choose a husband or wife is to be presented once a month.

The bureau of free love is autonomous.

Men between the ages of 19 and 50 have the right to choose from among the registered women, even without the consent of the latter, in the interests of the State.

Children who are the issue of these unions are to become the property of the State. . . .

Mr. President, could anything be more horrible and shocking? It is astounding and beyond comprehension that such a state of affairs can exist in the world of today, in any country which has ever claimed to be even semicivilized. It is shocking beyond expression to every sense of decency. It is worse than the practices of the most barbarous tribes of darkest Africa. Even among them a sort of mating of the sexes, a crude form of matrimony, is recognized and upheld. This beats the heathen. This is recognized, legalized, universal prostitution. It sinks to a lower depth than dumb brutes. Russia is a disgrace to the world. . . .

The despots of Russia are doing their best to spread their vile system of anarchy to the entire world. They boast of it. Their minions have invaded this fair country and their seed sown here is bearing fruit.

In the last few months 3,000 arrests of radical Reds, agitators, and undesirable aliens have been made by agents of the Department of Justice, with a view to their deportation. I have no doubt all of them are highly undesirable and are guilty of disloyal activities. I have no doubt this country would be better off if all of them were deported to the countries from which they came or tied in bags and dumped into the middle of the ocean. . . .

The activities of those who would undermine and overturn our Government are undoubtedly increasing. They appear to go on with little check or hindrance. In my opinion the country is honeycombed underneath the

REVOLUTION IN RUSSIA

The Bolshevik Revolution of 1917 was the culmination of nearly a century of rebellion and insurrection in Russia.

In December 1825 a group of army officers from aristocratic families organized a rebellion. Influenced by the European Enlightenment, these "Decembrists" sought the establishment of a constitution, the abolition of serfdom, and the granting of basic freedoms. They were swiftly crushed by Tsar Nicholas I.

Rebellious activity continued throughout the early nineteenth century, intensifying during the 1860–1890 period. In 1860–1861 widespread student protests erupted. A major rebellion developed in Poland in 1863, and an attempt was made on the life of Tsar Alexander II in 1866. The 1870s saw the growth of populist and anarchist movements, partic-ularly that of the "People's Will" revolutionary organization, which finally succeeded in assassinating Alexander II in 1881.

The turmoil in Russia grew worse in the 1880s and 1890s as the industrial revolution exacerbated social strains. Strikes, student protests, peasant rebellions, and other disturbances continued to multiply. Revolutionary intellectuals fell mostly into the Social Democratic (Marxist) or Social Revolutionary (Populist) groups.

January 22, 1905, became known as "Bloody Sunday" after the police opened fire on a workers' demonstration. A massive general strike later that year forced Nicholas II to form a legislature (Duma), grant certain civil liberties, and generally transform Russia from an absolute monarchy into a limited, constitutional monarchy.

The chaos, hunger, and suffering of World War I greatly increased popular dissatisfaction, and the Tsar's regime fell in March 1917. At this time the Bolsheviks represented only one group within the Social Democratic party. The "provisional" government that emerged, headed by Alexander Kerensky and praised by the West for its democratic principles, decided to continue Russia's involvement in the war. Suffering was prolonged, and the well-organized Bolsheviks, led by Vladimir Lenin, seized power in November 1917. However, the outcome of the Bolshevik Revolution was not finally settled until 1921. After nearly four more years of civil war between Bolsheviks ("Reds") and various counter-revolutionary ("White") groups, Lenin's Bolsheviks emerged unchallenged.

surface with the vicious activities of hydraheaded monsters and cunning plotters, who are scattering the poison of their malignant virus and working day and night for the overthrow of the best Government which the world has ever seen, where more liberty is given to the masses, more freedom to its citizens, more rights to its workingmen, more privileges to the whole populace than in any other Government under the sun. In my opinion this country is reeking and seething with the machinations of disloyalty, sedition, and bolshevism. Their proponents are becoming bold. They have defenders and sympathizers in high places.

While many Americans were caught up in such fantastic rhetoric, more practical issues demanded attention. Most distressing to the Western Allies was that Russia, their erstwhile friend in the war against Germany, was pursuing a separate peace. Without an active Eastern (Russian) front, Germany would be free to shift many troops to face the French, British, and Americans in the West. Thus, the Allies responded

Despite hostile government relations, during the famine of 1922, Americans such as George A. McKlintock, an inspector for the non-governmental American Relief Administration (above left), provided aid to starving Soviet children.

Bettman Archive.

with hostility, at first refusing even to recognize the new Soviet government. Later, and less well known in the U.S., the Allied powers (the "Entente") intervened in the civil war in Russia on the side of the "white" counterrevolutionaries. Bowing to considerable pressure from the British and French, President Woodrow Wilson reluctantly directed American troops to participate in the intervention. Although the "red" Bolsheviks ultimately prevailed, the experience of the intervention had a powerful effect on Soviet attitudes toward its security and the West. This is shown in the following excerpt from a 1940 Soviet dictionary.

Politicheskii Slovar' (Political Dictionary) (Moscow, 1940), p. 217.

ntervention: Military intervention, armed interference of one or several states in the internal affairs of another state, usually to suppress a revolution. In 1918–1920, Britain, France, Japan (up to October 1922), the U.S.A. and other countries tried by means of military invasion to overthrow the Soviet regime and restore capitalism in the Soviet land. The interventionists landed their troops in many areas of the Soviet land, formed and supported White Guard bands [see "Revolution in Russia" on page 19], supplying them with money, arms, and military instructions, until they were defeated by the Red Army and expelled from the borders.

With the Armistice in Europe, the Allies no longer worried about Russian cooperation against the Germans. And as it became clear that the new Soviet regime was barely holding onto power at home, fears about the Bolsheviks fomenting revolution abroad eased. Over time, with more and better information about events in the Soviet Union, American attitudes grew more complex. In the early 1920s, for example, news about famine in the aftermath of the Revolution and Civil War evoked sympathy. The following is a report of this famine from a contemporary American observer.

1926

Stalin consolidates power

1928–1929

First Five-Year Plan; forced collectivization of farms begins

1929–1933

Rapid industrialization underway; famine again as peasants resist collectivization; agricultural production plummets

We started from Moscow for our trip down into Samara, the largest city affected by the famine. It is situated on the Volga, and is a city of about 300,000 inhabitants, now very much increased in population by the refugees who are constantly pouring in from the country regions. Passing on to Buzuluk, a town formerly containing 20,000 people, now reduced to 12,000 because of the flight of those who could reach Siberia, we traveled out through the country regions.

I could hear the children crying two blocks away as I approached one of the homes for abandoned children in Samara, the central city of the famine area of Russia. A steady wail that kept up like a moan grew louder as we got nearer. The nurses could do nothing except to go around every morning and separate the babies that were going to die that day; and they went around at different times later and felt them to see if they were cold. In the evening those who had died during the day were gathered together and placed in heaps outside the building. A garbage-cart stopped each night and the baby bodies were loaded in. The garbage-cart stopped in the same way before all of the children's institutions in Samara and the other cities in the Volga region.

Children's homes, which are emptied of dead babies only to be refilled by the constant flow of abandoned children from the country; men and women and young children falling dead on the street from hunger; farm machinery, which in Russia is more precious than human life at the present time, lying scrapped by the roadside and rusting to pieces, tell the story of the extent and horror of the famine which is destroying the lives of 15,000,000 people in the greatest grain belt of Russia. . . .

The steppe ordinarily has no trees; it is a level, slightly rolling plain, with village after village scattered about five or ten miles apart. This fall it looked as though a prairie fire had swept over it. Farms and areas which are usually green or golden with harvest were burned almost black. What grass had grown was only a stunted growth on the surface of the ground. Every few rods as we went along we would scare away the carrion birds which were feasting on the carcasses of the dead horses and dogs that had died along the roadside. There was a continuous stream of refugees going our way, and we passed others going in the opposite direction. They did not much care which way they were going — they were just going to search for food.

I talked with the Russian priest and asked if next March would not be the worst month for them. He answered, "No, I think not. This month

Report of Anna Haines, American Friends Service Committee, 1922, as cited in Janet G. Vaillant and John Richards, *From Russia to USSR* (Wellesley Hills, MA: Independent School Press, 1985), pp. 216–218.

(September) we will be eating the vegetables and the watermelons and the rinds. In October there will still be the grass, and we can make the grass pancakes. In November, when the snow comes, [and] we can no longer get anything from the fields, we will still have our little reserve of a few potatoes or a little bit of grass flour. In December people will begin to die, and by the first of the year every bit of the reserve will be gone. In March there will be no one alive in the village."

While American organizations and individuals (notably the American Friends Service Committee and future President Herbert Hoover as head of the American Relief Administration) provided aid to victims of this famine, official American attitudes remained hostile. By the end of the 1920s, the U.S. was the only major nation that still refused to recognize the Soviet government. However, as news of the famine faded from the headlines and Joseph Stalin (Lenin's successor) announced ambitious plans for industrial growth, the ideals of the "great Soviet experiment" aroused the curiosity of many Americans. With the onset of the Great Depression, many looked at the apparent successes of the Soviet Five-Year Plan with admiration. Writer Malcolm Cowley describes the attitudes of many American intellectuals toward the U.S.S.R. during the depression years.

Malcolm Cowley, *The Dream of Golden Mountains: Remembering the 1930s* (New York: Penguin Books, 1964), pp. 34–35.

Marx's plans for reorganizing society were . . . being tested in Russia, a vast country that resembled our own in its pioneering spirit. Apparently their success had been amazing. A year before the crash in Wall Street, Russia had adopted her Five Year Plan, the first attempt in history to control in advance the economic output and living standards of a nation. Reports of its progress had been appearing not only in popular magazines but also in widely read books like *New Russia's Primer*, distributed in 1931 by the Book-of-the-Month Club, and in impressive films like Eisenstein's *The Old and the New*. Those were the Russian years in middle-class circles. . . .

Everybody quarreled about Russia, and almost everybody wanted to see and judge the new civilization for himself. Amtorg, the Soviet trading corporation that served as an informal consulate in those days before this country had recognized the Russian government, was receiving 350 applications a day from Americans eager to work for the Five Year Plan. The burden of most reports about the Plan was that it had enabled Russia to move in an opposite direction from the rest of the world. Under capitalism, everything had been going downhill; less and less of every vital commodity was being distributed each year. Under communism, everything was climbing dizzily upward; each year there was more wheat, more steel, more machinery, more electric power, and there was an unfailing market for everything that could be produced. Nobody walked the streets looking for a job. Under communism, it seemed that the epic of American pioneering was being repeated, not for the profit of a few robber barons, but for the people as a whole.

It is true that stories of a different sort were also coming out of Russia. Some of the newspapers reported that the fine new Russian factories were being wrecked by mismanagement and deliberate sabotage. In the winter of 1932–33 they reported that the result of collectivizing the Russian farms had been a famine [more devastating than the one in the 1920s] in the Ukraine with millions of peasants starving to death. Other millions, they claimed, had been reduced to slavery in labor camps — but were reports like these to be accepted? Many writers remembered that the newspapers, particularly those in the Hearst chain, had a long record of printing falsehoods about the Communists. There was undoubtedly much suffering in Russia, the writers said among themselves, and they were ready to admit that most of the unemployed in America got more to eat than skilled workers in Russia. But Americans, they also said, had to face the prospect of eating less and less as their savings were exhausted, whereas the Russians were fighting and suffering to build a world in which no one would go hungry.

Since 1917, fears that the spread of communism would destroy Western civilization have contributed to American attitudes toward the Soviet Union.

Gale, *Los Angeles Times*.

The U.S. finally extended full diplomatic recognition to the Soviet Union in 1933, and the Soviets joined the League of Nations in 1934. By this time Stalin was firmly in control of the Soviet state, and his programs for collectivized agriculture and massive industrialization were well underway. The 1930s were also a time of terror in the Soviet Union as Stalin had millions arrested or killed in a purge of any actual or imagined opposition to his absolute control. The height of this terror was reached with a series of "show trials" (see page 25) in 1936–1938, in which old Bolsheviks and former comrades of Lenin gave forced confessions to charges of conspiracies and sabotage against the Soviet Union. As the

1942–1943

Battle of Stalingrad; German invasion stopped

1944

German troops pushed back through Eastern Europe by Soviet Army

1945

February: Allied Conference on postwar agreements in Yalta attended by Roosevelt, Stalin, and Churchill

following dispatches from former U.S. Ambassador Joseph Davies show, many contemporary observers of the show trials actually believed the fantastic fabrications that Stalin used as a pretext for purging the Soviet government of his political rivals.

Joseph E. Davies, *Mission to Moscow* (New York: Pocket Books, 1943), pp. 235–238.

March 8, 1938: For the last week, I have been attending daily sessions of the Bukharin treason trial. No doubt you have been following it in the press. It is terrific. I have found it of much intellectual interest, because it brings back into play all the old critical faculties involved in assessing the credibility of witnesses and sifting the wheat from the chaff — the truth from the false — which I was called upon to use for so many years in the trial of cases, myself.

All the fundamental weaknesses and vices of human nature — personal ambitions at their worst — are shown up in the proceedings. They disclose the outlines of a plot which came very near to being successful in bringing about the overthrow of this government.

This testimony now makes clear what we could not understand about what happened last spring and summer. You will recall that the folks at the chancery were telling us of extraordinary activity around the Kremlin, when the gates were closed to the public; that there were indications of much agitation and a changing of the character of the soldiers on guard. The new guards, you will remember we were told, consisted almost entirely of soldiers recruited from Georgia, Stalin's native land.

The extraordinary testimony of Krestinsky, Bukharin, and the rest would appear to indicate that the Kremlin's fears were well justified. For it now seems that a plot existed in the beginning of November, 1936, to project a coup d'etat, with Tukhachevsky at its head, for May of the following year. Apparently it was touch and go at that time whether it actually would be staged.

But the government acted with great vigor and speed. The Red Army generals were shot and the whole party organization was purged and thoroughly cleansed. Then it came out that quite a few of those at the top were seriously infected with the virus of the conspiracy to overthrow the government, and were actually working with the Secret Service organizations of Germany and Japan.

The situation explains the present official attitude of hostility toward

1945

April: U.S. and Soviet armies meet on the Elbe; Roosevelt dies

1947

Truman Doctrine ("containment") announced

1948

Soviets blockade Berlin; U.S. airlifts supplies; Communist coup in Czechoslovakia

STALIN'S TERROR

The period from 1934 to 1939 was a time of unparalleled terror in the Soviet Union. Beginning with the assassination of popular Leningrad party boss Sergei Kirov, Stalin swiftly eliminated all opposition to his rule and every challenge to his authority. The most visible aspect of the purges was the well-publicized show trials of old Bolshevik leaders, in which evidence consisted solely of forced confessions to bizarre international plots and intrigues. In addition to Stalin's rivals in the Party, millions of ordinary citizens were swept away as well. The following are some figures on the purges.

Arrests:
4–8 million

Executions:
800,000

Jailed or imprisioned in labor camps:
7,200,000

Standard camp sentence:
10 years

Death rate in labor camps:
Over 1,000,000 per year (10%–20% annually)

Party victims:
70% of the 1934 Central Committee by 1939

Military victims:
3 of 5 marshals, 13 of 15 army commanders, 30 of 58 division commanders

The pattern of the terror is described below by Sovietologist Merle Fainsod:

The arrest of an important figure was followed by the seizure of the entourage which surrounded him. The apprehension of the entourage led to the imprisonment of their friends and acqaintances. The endless chain of involvements and associations threatened to encompass the entire strata of Soviet society. Fear of arrest, exhortations to vigilance, and perverted ambition unleashed new floods of denunciations, which generated their own avalanche of cumulative interrogations and detentions. . . . The vast resources of the NKVD [security police, KGB today] were concentrated on one objective—to document the existence of a huge conspiracy to undermine Soviet power. The extraction of real confessions to imaginary crimes became a major industry. Under the zealous and ruthless ministrations of NKVD examiners, millions of innocents were transformed into traitors, terrorists, and enemies of the people.

Merle Fainsod, *How Russia Is Ruled* (Cambridge: Harvard University Press, 1963), pp. 439–440.

1949

Soviet atomic bomb tested; Communist victory in China

1950

Korean War begins; Senator Joseph McCarthy charges State Department riddled with Communists

1953

Soviet H-bomb tested; Stalin dies

> **What historical and cultural forces motivate Soviet internal and international behavior? American behavior?**

foreigners, the closing of various foreign consulates in this country, and the like. Quite frankly, we can't blame the powers-that-be much for reacting in this way if they believed what is now being divulged at the trial. . . .

March 17, 1938: I have the honor to report that this confirms cable sent in confidential code with reference to the judgment of the court in the so-called Bukharin mass treason trial:

Paraphrase of the cable is as follows:

On March 13, 1938, at approximately five o'clock in the morning, all of the defendants in the trial were adjudged guilty and the sentences were imposed. Three of the defendants were condemned to imprisonment and the remainder to death through shooting. Eight of the most prominent former members of the Soviet government, including a former premier, six former cabinet officers, one of the most promising party leaders and member of the Politburo, and also a former president of one of the constituent republics were among those comdemned to be shot. Condemned to imprisonment were a former Ambassador to England and France, a former Counselor of the Soviet Embassy in Berlin, and one famous heart specialist.

Notwithstanding a prejudice arising from the confession evidence and a prejudice against a judicial system which affords practically no protection for the accused, after daily observation of the witnesses, their manner of testifying, the unconscious corroborations which developed, and other facts in the course of the trial, together with others of which a judicial notice could be taken, it is my opinion so far as the political defendants are concerned sufficient crimes under Soviet law, among those charged in the indictment, were established by the proof beyond a reasonable doubt to justify the verdict of guilty of treason and the adjudication of the punishment provided by Soviet criminal statutes.

With the rise to power of Hitler and Mussolini in the 1930s, American interest in Soviet domestic issues gave way to worry about the possibilities of war in Europe. American supporters and critics of the U.S.S.R. alike were shocked by the announcement, in August 1939, of a Non-Aggression Pact between Hitler and Stalin. (Under the secret terms of this pact Stalin and Hitler agreed not to attack each other and to divide Poland between them.) Americans who had seen the Soviet Union as a steadfast opponent of fascism felt betrayed; others saw in the pact more proof of the fundamentally untrustworthy character of the U.S.S.R.

The Soviets had another perspective. They saw the Non-Aggression Pact with Hitler as a necessary evil forced upon them by the policies of England, France, and the U.S., embodied a year earlier in the Munich Agreement. While British Prime Minister Neville Chamberlain proclaimed that this agreement, by appeasing Hitler with the Sudeten region of Czechoslovakia, had brought "peace in our time," the Soviets felt that the Western powers had betrayed the Czechs in an attempt to turn Hitler's ambitions eastward, toward the U.S.S.R. In the Soviet view, the Non-Aggression Pact between Hitler and Stalin, far from being a betrayal or capitulation to Nazism, was an attempt to forestall the inevitable Nazi attack on Russia. (Regardless of Stalin's intentions, Hitler's interpretation of the pact — Soviet approval to invade Poland — is seen by many as the key event that hastened the war.)

Below is a Soviet view of the Munich "betrayal," as reflected in a speech by Stalin.

We are witnessing an open redivision of the world and spheres of influence at the expense of the nonaggressive states, without the least attempt at resistance, and even with a certain connivance on their part. Incredible, but true. To what are we to attribute this one-sided and strange character of the new imperialist war? How is it that the nonaggressive countries, which possess such vast opportunities, have so easily and without resistance abandoned their positions and their obligations to please the aggressors? Is it to be attributed to the weakness of the nonaggressive states? Of course not! Combined, the nonaggressive democratic states are unquestionably stronger than the fascist states, both economically and militarily. To what then are we to attribute the systematic concessions made by these states to the aggressors? . . .

The chief reason is that the majority of the nonaggressive countries, particularly Britain and France, have rejected the [Soviet-proposed] policy of collective security, the policy of collective resistance to aggressors, and have taken up a position of nonintervention, a position of "neutrality." Formally speaking, the policy of nonintervention might be defined as follows: "Let each country defend itself against the aggressors as it likes and as best it can. That is not our affair. We shall trade both with the aggressors and with their victims." But actually speaking, the policy of nonintervention means conniving at aggression, giving

Joseph Stalin, "Report to the Eighteenth Congress of the Communist Party of the Soviet Union," March 10, 1939, as quoted in Alvin Z. Rubinstein, *The Foreign Policy of the Soviet Union* (New York: Random House, 1968), pp. 146–148.

Championing Allied cooperation, this Soviet war poster proclaimed, "A THUNDEROUS BLOW."

Poster by Kukryniksy, courtesy of U.S.S.R. Embassy, Washington, DC.

free rein to war, and, consequently, transforming the war into a world war. The policy of nonintervention reveals an eagerness, a desire, not to hinder the aggressors in their nefarious work: not to hinder Japan, say, from embroiling herself in a war with China, or, better still, with the Soviet Union; not to hinder Germany, say, from enmeshing herself in European affairs, from embroiling herself in a war with the Soviet Union; to allow all the belligerents to sink deeply into the mire of war, to encourage them surreptitiously in this; to allow them to weaken and exhaust one another; and then, when they have become weak enough, to appear on the scene with fresh strength, to appear, of course, "in the interests of peace," and to dictate conditions to the enfeebled belligerents.

Cheap and easy!

1959
Khrushchev visits U.S.

1960
May: U-2 spy plane shot down over U.S.S.R.; Sino-Soviet split widens

1961
April: Yuri Gagarin becomes first man in space

. . . take Germany, for instance. They let her have Austria, despite the undertaking to defend her independence; they let her have the Sudeten region; they abandoned Czechoslovakia to her fate, thereby violating all their obligations; and then they began to lie vociferously in the press about "the weakness of the Russian army," "the demoralization of the Russian air force," and "riots" in the Soviet Union, egging on the Germans to march farther east, promising them easy pickings, and prompting them: "Just start war on the Bolsheviks, and everything will be all right." It must be admitted that this looks very much like egging on and encouraging the aggressor.

As Americans, do we accept as credible the historical forces that motivate Soviet behavior?

Responding to the German invasion of Russia in June 1941, and the Japanese attack on Pearl Harbor later the same year, the U.S. and the Soviet Union quickly found themselves allied in a common struggle. The years of the Second World War saw more U.S.-Soviet cooperation than ever before or since. Although mutual suspicions were hardly eliminated, popular attitudes on both sides were considerably more generous than ever before. This is shown in the following letter, written to the editor of *The Arizona Republic,* and in George Kennan's description of Soviet gratitude toward Americans upon the German surrender in 1945.

n the midst of the childish babblings and thoughtless criticisms of some of our leading newspapers, the Russian army has again gone into action. The truth cannot seem to penetrate the brain of some of our war reporters, for even now a few of them are trying to belittle the fighting of the brave Soviet armies, who already have driven back the German "supermen" more than a thousand miles.

There has seemed to be an effort to make the people of America believe that these undemocratic Communists, who already have done more than the rest of the united nations to rid the world of the Nazi plague, were not doing their share even though they were licking the tar out of the Germans in Hungary and elsewhere. Just because of a minor setback on our western front, we began to blame the Russians for the lack of an offensive on the Polish front. Let us not forget that it was Russia who waited and fought for three years before we were able to help them with a second front.

At the present time it is said that they are making such good progress

John L. Billings (Globe, AZ), letter to the editor, *The Arizona Republic,* February 4, 1945, p. 5.

1961

August: Berlin Wall erected

1962

October: Cuban missile crisis

1963

November: John F. Kennedy assassinated

because the Germans are retreating. Yes, they are retreating and running so fast that their army is being destroyed by the tens of thousands. They are retreating, but leaving their war implements behind them; they are retreating because they cannot withstand the grind of the mighty Soviet war machine.

Let us not forget the sacrifices and bravery of the Russian people, even though they do not have the same form of government as we have. There is enough room in this world for all of us, so let's stop this thoughtless criticizing and be a little more friendly.

George F. Kennan, *Memoirs: 1925–1950* (Boston: Little, Brown, 1967), pp. 240–242.

It was May 9, one day after V-E Day in the west, before the Russians, still suspicious lest the Germans continue resistance in the east even after surrendering to the British and Americans, consented to accept the fact that the war in Europe was over and to let their people know it. The news got about in Moscow in the very early hours of the morning of the tenth; and by daybreak a holiday mood so exuberant as to defy all normal disciplinary restraints was gripping the city. . . .

About ten o'clock in the morning, contingents of young people, apparently students, marching with songs and banners along the street before these buildings, spied the Allied flags on the National Hotel and burst into cordial cheers. Then, as they moved beyond the hotel, they discovered the Stars and Stripes, reacted with what appeared to be in most instances a surprised delight, stopped their march, and settled down to demonstrate before the embassy building feelings that were obviously ones of almost delirious friendship. The square before the building was commodious — it could have held two hundred thousand people — and soon our initial well-wishers were augmented by thousands of others, who joined in the friendly cheering and waving and showed not the slightest desire to move on. We were naturally moved and pleased by this manifestation of public feeling, but were at a loss to know how to respond to it. If any of us ventured into the street, he was immediately seized, tossed enthusiastically into the air, and passed on friendly hands over the heads of the crowd, to be lost, eventually, in a confused orgy of good feeling somewhere on its outer fringes. Few of us were anxious to court this experience, so we lined the balconies and waved back as bravely as we could.

As a gesture of reciprocation, I sent one of our people across the roof of the National Hotel and procured from the hotel a Soviet flag, which we

hung out together with our own. This produced new roars of approval and enthusiasm. But it did not seem enough. Being at that time charge d'affaires (the ambassador was away), I thought it incumbent on me to say at least a word or two in appreciation. . . . I went down to the first floor and climbed out onto the pedestal of one of the great columns that lined the front of the building. With me among others (for some cock-eyed reason buried in the agreeable confusions of the day) came a sergeant of the military mission in uniform — a man who was, as I understood it, a preacher in real life. Our appearance produced new transports of approval on the part of the crowd. The police, who had been holding the people away from the walls of the building, and one party agitator who had obviously been sent to try to assume leadership of the people and get them to move on, were now good-naturedly shoved aside, and the crowd pushed over the little barrier that lined the sidewalk, and onto the grass plots at the foot of the building, so that they now surround the pedestal. I shouted to them in Russian: "Congratulations on the day of victory. All honor to the Soviet allies" — which seemed to me to be about all I could suitably say. At this, roaring with apprecia-

War veterans marching in Red Square during the International Workers, or May Day, Parade provide yet another reminder to the Soviets of World War II.
SIPA/Special Features.

1964
Khrushchev ousted from power by Politburo rivals

1968
August: Soviets invade Czechoslovakia, end liberalization

1969
July: U.S. Apollo 11 lands on the moon

tion, they hoisted up a Soviet soldier on their hands to the point where he would reach the pedestal. He pulled himself up into our company, kissed and embraced the startled sergeant, and pulled him relentlessly down to the waiting arms of the crowd. There, bobbing helplessly over a sea of hands, he rapidly receded from our view (and did not come back until the next day, I was told). I myself successfully escaped back into the building.

All day long, and well into the evening, this great crowd remained, waving and cheering, before the building. The Soviet authorities were naturally not entirely pleased with this situation, particularly because this was, so far as we could learn, the only place in Moscow where any demonstration of anything resembling these dimensions took place. A single polite though slightly suspicious cheer on the part of the crowd, accompanied by evidences of determination to destroy the "remnants of fascism" (meaning any form of opposition to Soviet political purposes), might, one feels, have been considered in order, but certainly not this warmth, this friendliness, this enthusiasm, demonstrated before the representatives of a government of whose iniquities, as a bourgeois power, Soviet propagandists had spent more than two decades trying to persuade people. It is not hard to imagine what mortification this must have brought to both party and police. Without their solicitious prearrangement not even a sparrow had fallen in a Moscow street for twenty-seven years, and now, suddenly — this! Continued efforts were made to get the crowd to move on. A band-stand was even hastily erected and a brass band put into operation on the other side of the square. But it was all to no avail. The crowd stayed. We ourselves were even a little embarrassed; we had no desire to be the sources of such trouble on a day of common rejoicing. We had done nothing, God knows, to invite the demonstration, or to encourage its prolongation, once it had started. But we were even more helpless than the authorities.

Despite such seemingly auspicious outpourings of goodwill, U.S.-Soviet relations began deteriorating even as the war was ending. The first area of conflict was Eastern Europe. In February of 1945, at a meeting in Yalta of the "Big Three" allied leaders (Franklin Roosevelt, Winston Churchill, and Stalin), the Soviets agreed to hold "free and unfettered elections" in East European countries occupied by the Red Army. Instead, the Soviets installed Communist governments throughout East-

1972

Nixon meets Brezhnev in Moscow; SALT I arms-control treaty signed; U.S.-Soviet trade agreement signed

1973

Brezhnev visits Washington

1974

Congress enacts Jackson-Vanik Amendment linking trade relations to Jewish emigration

U.S. POLICIES TOWARD THE U.S.S.R., 1917–PRESENT

Years	Presidents	Policy	Key Points
1917–1932	Wilson-Hoover	Nonrecognition	U.S. does not recognize Soviet regime until 1933.
1933–1940	Roosevelt	Normal diplomatic relations	U.S. sends first ambassador to Moscow in 1934.
1941–1945	Roosevelt-Truman	Alliance	U.S. and U.S.S.R. cooperate in Hitler's defeat; U.S. sends Lend-Lease aid.
1945–1946	Truman	Transition	U.S. disillusioned as Soviets consolidate power in Eastern Europe; Communists gain in China.
1947–1952	Truman	Containment	Truman Doctrine pledges to contain Communist expansion; NATO formed; Korean War.
1953–1962	Eisenhower-Kennedy	Cold war	Secretary of State Dulles advocates challenging Soviet power; U.S. combats Soviet influence in the Middle East, South Asia, and Latin America; Berlin Wall and Cuban missile crises.
1963–1968	Kennedy-Johnson	Thaw	Relations improve slowly; Limited Test Ban and Outer Space treaties signed.
1969–1978	Nixon-Carter	Detente	SALT I and ABM treaties signed; Jackson-Vanik amendment links trade to Soviet emigration policy; Soviet "adventurism" in Africa denounced.
1979–1986	Carter-Reagan		SALT II signed but not ratified by U.S.; Soviets invade Afghanistan; arms-control process disrupted.

ern Europe. In the minds of many Americans, communism replaced fascism as the threat to freedom and democracy in the world. Although some Americans feared that a showdown with the U.S.S.R. was unavoidable, a different view is reflected in the following article from the *Woman's Home Companion.*

As part of the Allied agreements reached at Yalta after World War II, Germany was divided into four zones: Soviet, American, British, and French.

Thomas, *The Detroit News* (1949).

Woman's Home Companion, vol. LXXV (March 1948), p. 4, as quoted in Peter G. Filene, *American Views of Soviet Russia* (Homewood, IL: Dorsey Press, 1968), pp. 235–237.

IS WAR INEVITABLE?

The most dangerous habit in America today is the habitual talk of an inevitable war with Russia. We hear such talk everywhere — on the street, in stores, in trains and buses, at lectures, at the dinner table, even in church.

You may say words are only words. They break no bones and they will never harm us. But this is to take the force of mental habits too lightly. . . . The talk of war may become inseparable from the event for which it is preparing the ground. By dwelling so long on it, people may be ready to welcome it as a relief from suspense and as a fulfillment of expectation.

We are not implying that all is well in our relations with Russia. Obviously it is not. American-Russian relations have deteriorated badly in the postwar years. . . .

It is true that the Russians have thrown their weight around in a way that makes international understanding and cooperation extremely difficult. Incidentally all American leaders and diplomats have not behaved like angels either. In an effort to restrain the expansion of Russian power, many have tightened the screws hard on Russia and its sphere of

1974

August: Nixon resigns; Ford meets Brezhnev in Vladivostok

1975

July: Apollo-Soyuz flight

1979

Carter and Brezhnev sign SALT II; Soviets invade Afghanistan

influence. What is going on looks like a struggle for power between the only two remaining Great Powers in the world. Each fears the power, the ideas, the social system of the other. Only the naive can shut their eyes to these facts. . . .

This is a time for the kind of sanity and common sense on which Americans usually pride themselves. The tensions in this world are bad enough without increasing them by irresponsible talk.

The Communist coup in Czechoslovakia (1948), the Berlin blockade and airlift (1948–1949), the Communist takeover in China (1949), the successful Soviet test of an atomic bomb (1949), and the North Korean invasion of South Korea (1950) effectively froze debate in America about communism and the Soviet Union. American-Soviet relations were plunged fully into the cold war. U.S. domestic politics and foreign policy both evidenced the common perception that communism and internal subversion by Communists, even more than Soviet military power, was a mortal threat to American democracy.

Preventing further Communist expansion was seen as the minimal goal of American policy; some, such as Secretary of State John Foster Dulles, advocated a more ambitious strategy to "roll back" Soviet gains. The following speech, given by Francis Cardinal Spellman in 1954, typifies this position.

"Despite such seemingly auspicious outpourings of goodwill, U.S.-Soviet relations began deteriorating even as the war was ending."

For too long we have looked upon each act of Communist aggression as a self-contained conflict where we should have recognized each one as a carefully calculated incident in a world-wide struggle that enlists the zeal, energy, and discipline of Communists everywhere.

What we fail so tragically to realize is that communism has a world plan and it has been following a carefully set up time-table for the achievement of that plan. Red rulers know what they want with terrible clarity; determined to get what they want with violent consistency. Up to the present the Communist advances have concerned us, as Americans, only insofar as it [sic] has involved nations and peoples for whom we have the deepest sympathy and most sincere admiration. We are appalled at their enslavement but our sorrow is as nothing compared to the infamies and agonies inflicted upon the hapless victims of Red Russia's bestial tyranny. However, time is running out for us also, because given the

Francis Cardinal Spellman, Archbishop of New York, "Communism Has a World Plan: Time Is Running Out for Us," a speech to the American Legion Convention, August 30, 1954.

FACTS AND FIGURES ON THE U.S.S.R.

Land mass	8.6 million square miles (16% of world total)
Time zones	11
Population	275 million
Population distribution	64% urban, 36% rural
Major cities	Moscow (8.2 M), Leningrad (4.7 M), Kiev (2.5 M) Tashkent (1.9 M)
Nationalities	Over 150
Languages and major dialects	Over 150
Ethnic composition	72% Slavic, 16% Turkic, 3% Caucasian, 2% Latvian/ Lithuanian, 2% Iranian, etc.
Religions	70% atheist, 18% Russian Orthodox, 9% Muslim, 3% Jewish; also Protestant, Georgian Orthodox, Roman Catholic
Life expectancy	Female, 71 years; male, 60 years
Infant mortality	31 per 1000 births (approximately)
Adult literacy	98%
Television ownership	300 sets per 1000 people
Major natural resources	Oil, gas, coal, iron, phosphates, manganese, zinc, other ores and minerals
Agriculture	27% of land cultivated; products include wheat, rye, oats, potatoes, beets, linseed, sunflower seed, cotton, flax, livestock
Major exports	Oil, gas, coal, metal ores, fertilizer, lumber, cotton, machinery, weapons
Average annual per capita income	$5,750
National holidays	Woman's Day (March 8), May Day (May 1), Victory Day (May 9), Revolution Day (November 7), New Year's Day (January 1)
Popular sports and games	Soccer, ice hockey, chess, basketball
Political system	Communist party rule

See maps on pages 134 and 141.

1980

U.S. boycotts Moscow Olympics

1981

Solidarity suppressed by Polish government

1983

September: Soviets shoot down Korean airliner

present pace of the Communist advance, it cannot be long before its encircling pincers will be turning upon ourselves. . . .

Dear friends and fellow Americans, I speak to you in the frankest terms. . . . Your deep concern lest subversive groups undermine our American way of life has been manifested for many years, even when such manifestation exposed you to ridicule and abuse. You have known the menace of communism and you have alerted your members to it. However, there is a vast number of our countrymen who live in complete indifference to the terrifying fact that communism will settle for nothing less than the domination of the whole wide world.

Thirty-five years ago Lenin made this prophecy:

"First we will take Eastern Europe; then the masses of Asia. Then we will encircle the United States of America which will be the last bastion of capitalism. We will not have to attack; it will fall like an overripe fruit into our hands. . . ." [*Ed. note:* Although these words are still occasionally cited, there is no evidence that they are Lenin's.]

It may be that the challenge of evil totalitarianism will be faced by us sooner than we think, and in that event we will need all the strength that our prayers and sacrifices can bring to us. The prophecy of Lenin should at least have the merit of putting us on our guard. We remember how paralyzing a blow was struck at our nation in the surprise attack at Pearl Harbor. . . .

The danger of another Pearl Harbor embracing the whole American people is definitely possible and possibly imminent. . . .

Americans must not be lulled into sleep by indifference nor be beguiled by the prospect of peaceful coexistence with Communists. How can there be peaceful coexistence between two parties if one of them is continually clawing at the throat of the other, continually threatening, continually committing actions which are designed to destroy life in the other party? How does one peacefully coexist with men who mouth words of peace while waging treacherous war; men who wear the trappings of civilization while they indulge in the techniques of barbarism? It is ignorance of a fatal kind which prompts the illusion that free men can peacefully coexist with Communists.

During the early 1950s Senator Joseph P. McCarthy generated widespread anti-Communist hysteria with unsupported and slanderous accusations of Communist infiltration in the U.S. government.

Courtesy of *Wheeling West Virginia Intelligencer.*

Stalin's death in 1953 set the stage for a gradual improvement in U.S.-Soviet relations. Although it took several years for him to emerge as the undisputed leader, once in control Nikita Khrushchev moved swiftly to reverse the worst excesses of the Stalin period. Khrushchev's policy of "de-Stalinization" included a less paranoid attitude toward the U.S. and the adoption of the policy of "peaceful coexistence" with the West. From the American perspective, better relations with the U.S.S.R. were blocked by such Soviet actions as the invasion of Hungary and construction of the Berlin Wall. As the following excerpt from Khrushchev's memoir shows, however, the Soviets blame the U.S. for continuing the cold war, particularly through acts such as the overflights of U–2 spy planes.

Strobe Talbott (trans. and ed.), *Khrushchev Remembers: The Last Testament* (Boston: Little, Brown, 1974), pp. 443–447.

We'd been acquainted with the U–2 [reconnaissance plane] for some time. On several occasions we'd protested its violations of our airspace, but each time the U.S. brushed our protests aside, saying that none of their planes were overflying our territory. We were more infuriated and disgusted every time a violation occurred. We did everything we could to intercept the U–2 and shoot it down with our fighters, but they couldn't reach the altitude the U–2 was flying at. As I recall, our fighters could climb only to 18,000 or 20,000 meters, while the U–2 operated at 21,000 meters. Fortunately, by that time, our surface-to-air missiles had already started rolling off the production line. It looked like they were going to be the answer to our problem. . . .

The latest flight, toward Sverdlovsk, was an especially deep penetration into our territory and therefore an especially arrogant violation of our sovereignty. We were sick and tired of these unpleasant surprises, sick and tired of being subjected to these indignities. They were making these flights to show up our impotence. Well, we weren't impotent any longer. . . .

[An American U–2, piloted by Gary Francis Powers, was shot down over Soviet territory in early May 1960. The Soviets did not announce that the pilot had been captured alive, and the U.S. apparently assumed that he had been killed.]

As long as the Americans thought the pilot was dead, they would keep putting out the story that perhaps the plane had accidentally strayed off course and had been shot down in the mountains on the Soviet side of the border.

Two or three days later, after they talked themselves out and got thoroughly wound up in this unbelievable story, we decided to tell the world what really happened. The time had come to pin down the Americans and expose their lies. I was authorized to make the statement. We laid out everything just as it had occurred: the plane's point of origin, its route, its destination, and its mission. . . .

America had been pursuing a two-faced policy. On the one hand, the U.S. had been approaching us with outstretched arms and all sorts of assurances about their peaceful intentions. On the other hand, they were stabbing us in the back. Fortunately, we caught them in the act and made the most of it. . . .

Once we had exposed them outright in their lie, the American press started saying that Eisenhower didn't know about these flights: they were the work of [CIA Director] Allen Dulles, the brother of the late Secretary of State, and Eisenhower would never have approved such tricks had Dulles ever reported them to him. This of course was the most reasonable explanation for an unreasonable action. It gave the President a chance to vindicate himself and save face in light of the meeting that was to take place in Paris. I went out of my way not to accuse the President in my own statements. . . .

But the Americans wouldn't let the matter rest there. One day in May we got a report that President Eisenhower had made a statement saying that he had known about the U–2 flight in advance and he had approved.

The Cuban missile crisis of October 1962 marked a turning point in U.S.-Soviet relations. The confrontation, which made the risks of nuclear war between the superpowers starkly apparent, shocked many Americans and led to a desire for less dangerous relations with the Soviet Union. President John F. Kennedy gave voice to this desire in 1963.

Let us reexamine our attitude toward the Soviet Union. It is discouraging to think that their leaders may actually believe what their propagandists write. It is discouraging to read a recent authoritative Soviet text on military strategy and find, on page after page, wholly baseless and incredible claims — such as the allegation that "American imperialist circles are preparing to unleash different types of wars . . . that there is a very real threat of a preventive war being unleashed by American imperialists against the Soviet Union . . . [and that] the political aims of the American imperialists are to enslave economically and politically the European and other capitalist countries . . . [and] to achieve world domination . . . by means of aggressive wars."

John F. Kennedy, "Toward a Strategy of Peace," Commencement Address at American University, June 10, 1963.

Truly as it was written long ago: "The wicked flee when no man pursueth." Yet it is sad to read these Soviet statements — to realize the extent of the gulf between us. But it is also a warning — a warning to the American people not to fall into the same trap as the Soviets, not to see only a distorted and desperate view of the other side, not to see conflict as inevitable, accommodation as impossible, and communication as nothing more than an exchange of threats.

No government or social system is so evil that its people must be considered as lacking in virtue. As Americans we find communism profoundly repugnant as a negation of personal freedom and dignity. But we can still hail the Russian people for their many achievements — in science and space, in economic and industrial growth, in culture and in acts of courage.

Among the many traits the peoples of our two countries have in common, none is stronger than our mutual abhorrence of war. Almost unique among the major world powers, we have never been at war with each other. And no nation in the history of battle ever suffered more than the Soviet Union suffered in the course of the Second World War. At least 20 million lost their lives. Countless millions of homes and farms were burned or sacked. A third of the nation's territory, including nearly two-thirds of its industrial base, was turned into a wasteland — a loss equivalent to the devastation of this country east of Chicago.

Today, should total war ever break out again — no matter how — our two countries could become the primary targets. It is an ironical but accurate fact that the two strongest powers are the two in the most danger of devastation. All we have built, all we have worked for, would be destroyed in the first 24 hours. And even in the cold war, which brings burdens and dangers to so many countries — including this nation's closest allies — our two countries bear the heaviest burdens. For we are both devoting massive sums of money to weapons that could be better devoted to combating ignorance, poverty, and disease. We are both caught up in a vicious and dangerous cycle in which suspicion on one side breeds suspicion on the other and new weapons beget counter-weapons.

In short, both the United States and its allies, and the Soviet Union and its allies, have a mutually deep interest in a just and genuine peace, and in halting the arms race. Agreements to this end are in the interests of the Soviet Union as well as ours, and even the most hostile nations can be relied upon to accept and keep those treaty obligations, and only those treaty obligations, which are in their own interest.

So let us not be blind to our differences, but let us also direct attention to our common interests and to the means by which those differences can be resolved. And if we cannot end now our differences, at least we can help make the world safe for diversity. For in the final analysis our most basic common link is that we all inhabit this planet. We all breathe the same air. We all cherish our children's future. And we are all mortal.

"She Might Have Invaded Russia"

The Czech experiment with political and economic reform (the "Prague Spring") was crushed by Warsaw Pact forces in 1968 for fear that it would spread throughout Eastern Europe and the Soviet Union.

From *The Herblock Gallery* (Simon and Schuster, 1968).

As U.S.-Soviet relations gradually improved throughout the 1960s, the two nations began to cooperate in many areas. Important arms control agreements (the Limited Test Ban, Antiballistic Missile, and SALT I treaties) were signed in 1963 and 1972, and the two superpowers expanded cultural and economic ties. Under President Richard Nixon and General Secretary Leonid Brezhnev, the U.S. and the U.S.S.R. accelerated this trend and embarked on the era of detente.

The rise and subsequent fall of detente presents a classic case study of the role of perceptions in U.S.-Soviet relations. In both nations there were (and still are) strong supporters and dedicated opponents of detente. The former group believes that despite the vast differences in our societies and governments, the U.S. and the U.S.S.R. can cooperate in many areas to the benefit of both. The latter group in both countries

Presidents Nixon, Ford, Carter, and Reagan have each met with their Soviet counterparts, Brezhnev and Gorbachev. Highly publicized summit meetings have sometimes led to formal agreements and at other times served as a way for superpower leaders to become acquainted.

Bettman Archive.

believes that the differences between the U.S. and U.S.S.R. are too fundamental to be overcome and that the best policy is to go it alone, pursuing national security unilaterally.

Various misperceptions contributed to the decline of detente. As Americans we may have failed to appreciate the extent to which the Soviets were deeply offended by what they saw as our self-righteous attitude. We underestimated the extent to which national pride plays a major role in Soviet behavior; even more than us, the Soviets seek status and recognition in the community of nations. The Jackson-Vanik amendment to the the 1972 Trade Agreement, which linked favorable trade status with increased Jewish emigration, was seen by the Soviets as (and may even have been intended by some to be) an insult. And although the amendment was the only obstacle to the agreements, which the Soviets sorely wanted, they could not countenance this degree of what they viewed as a moralizing interference in Soviet internal affairs. They seemed especially sensitive to such interference when the negotiations became public, as they did in this incident. Jewish emigration was curtailed, the trade agreement languished, and detente was dealt a crippling blow.

For their part the Soviets overestimated the extent to which American acceptance of the Soviet Union as a partner in detente implied American tolerance of other aspects of Soviet behavior. Although detente was already in jeopardy, the Soviets appeared genuinely surprised at the U.S. reaction to their invasion of Afghanistan. To the Soviets' thinking, Afghanistan was in their "backyard" and thus should have been of little concern and no threat to the U.S. They apparently did not expect that their invasion would so outrage and offend Americans that it would end any chance for U.S. ratification of the SALT II Treaty.

Many people, Soviet and American, expected too much of detente. It was misperceived as a new relationship when it was really something less — a different approach to an old relationship. Detente enthusiasts, Soviet and American, blurred differences between our two countries, each assuming that in time the other side would come around and "see us as we see ourselves." These inflated expectations could not be met, and this led (not surprisingly, in hindsight) to unnecessary disappointment. As much as the actual events, such misperceptions played a key role in the rise and fall of detente. What follows are two contrasting American views on the detente period of U.S.-Soviet relations.

Are Soviet and American reactions to each nation's attempts to influence the domestic policies of the other similar or different?

Many historians have noted that in their conduct of foreign policy Americans are much given to moralizing. . . .

The Kissinger-Nixon (or Nixon-Kissinger) mode of diplomacy is widely judged to have broken with this moralizing tradition. It is described as realistic, pragmatic, non-utopian, and non-ideological, basing itself on things as they are, not as we might

James Burnham, "Detente (Deletions)," *National Review,* August 2, 1974, p. 857.

have wished them to be. This is the frame within which Secretary Kissinger and the President motivate their policy of detente toward the two major Communist powers. Whether we like it or not, China and the Soviet Union are *there*. Though our system of government differs greatly from theirs, we should nevertheless try to develop relations with them that will further what we may assume to be common aims: specifically, to decrease the chance of nuclear war and to promote mutually beneficial trade. . . . [T]he Soviet government in no way exhibits the Nixon-Kissinger sort of qualms. Day after day, in the official press and

During the period of detente, the U.S. and the Soviet Union agreed to scientific exchanges, including the linking of the Soyuz and Apollo spacecraft in 1975.

N.A.S.A., Washington, DC.

"Turn Up The Cloud Machine, Angels Enter From The Left—"

broadcasts and through the global apparatus, harsh attacks on the policies and practices of the U.S. and on U.S. officials and citizens continue. The latest outburst in the official government newspaper *Izvestia* includes our poor liberals in the enemy list, along with "the military-industrial complex, anachronistic imperialist reaction, Zionist circles, professional anti-Communists, and antisemites [sic] of all breeds."

This asymmetry in the matter of speaking out parallels asymmetries observable in the strategic arms negotiations and in the trade deals. In each case the U.S. appears in the figure of the supplicant approaching hat in hand, eyes downcast, and voice humbly lowered.

The pomp and circumstance surrounding summits have seemed at times to overshadow the summits themselves.

Courtesy of Don Wright, *The Miami News.*

This administration has never had any illusions about the Soviet system. We have always insisted that progress in technical fields, such as trade, had to follow — and reflect — progress toward more stable international relations. We have maintained a strong military balance and a flexible defense posture as a buttress to stability. We have insisted that disarmament had to be mutual. We have judged movement in our relations with the Soviet Union not by atmospherics but by how well concrete problems are resolved and by whether there is responsible international conduct . . . .

Henry A. Kissinger, "Moral Purposes and Policy Choices," an address, *Department of State Bulletin*, vol. LXIX, no. 1792 (October 29, 1973), pp. 527–529.

SOVIET AND AMERICAN LEADERS, 1933–1986

	President			General Secretary	
Secretary of State		Ambassador to the U.S.S.R.	Foreign Minister		Ambassador to the U.S.
Franklin D. Roosevelt			*Joseph V. Stalin*		
Cordell Hull		William Bullitt	Maxim Litvinov		Alexander Troyanovsky
Edward Stettinius		Joseph Davies	Vyacheslav Molotov		Konstantin Oumansky
		Laurence Steinhardt	Andrei Vyshinsky		Maxim Litvinov
		William Standley			Andrei Gromyko
		Averell Harriman			Nikolai Novikov
					Alexander Panyushkin
					Georgi Zaroubin
Harry S. Truman					
James Byrnes		Averell Harriman			
George Marshall		Walter Smith			
Dean Acheson		Alan Kirk			
		George Kennan			
Dwight D. Eisenhower			*Nikita S. Khrushchev*		
John Dulles		Charles Bohlen	Vyacheslav Molotov		Georgi Zaroubin
Christian Herter		Lewellyn Thompson	Andrei Gromyko		Mikhail Menshikov
					Anatoli Dobrynin
John F. Kennedy					
Dean Rusk		Llewellyn Thompson			
		Foy Kohler			

On this basis we have succeeded in transforming U.S.-Soviet relations in many important ways. Our two countries have concluded a historic accord to limit strategic arms. We have substantially reduced the risk of direct U.S.-Soviet confrontation in crisis areas. The problem of Berlin has been resolved by negotiation. We and our allies have engaged the Soviet Union in negotiations on major issues of European security, including a reduction of military forces in central Europe. We have reached a series of bilateral agreements on cooperation — health, environment, space, science and technology, as well as trade. These accords are designed to create a vested interest in cooperation and restraint.

Until recently the goals of detente were not an issue. The necessity of

| President | | | General Secretary | |
Secretary of State	Ambassador to the U.S.S.R.		Foreign Minister	Ambassador to the U.S.
Lyndon B. Johnson				
Dean Rusk	Foy Kohler			
	Llewellyn Thompson		*Leonid I. Brezhnev*	
			Andrei Gromyko	Anatoli Dobrynin
Richard M. Nixon				
William Rogers	Jacob Beam			
Henry Kissinger	Walter Stoessel			
Gerald R. Ford				
Henry Kissinger	Walter Stoessel			
Jimmy E. Carter				
Cyrus Vance	Malcolm Toon			
Edmund Muskie	Thomas Watson			
Ronald W. Reagan				
Alexander Haig	Arthur Hartman		*Yuri V. Andropov*	
George Shultz			Andrei Gromyko	Anatoli Dobrynin
			Konstantin U. Chernenko	
			Andrei Gromyko	Anatoli Dobrynin
			Mikhail S. Gorbachev	
			Andrei Gromyko	Anatoli Dobrynin
			Eduard Shevardnadze	Yuri Dubinin

shifting from confrontation toward negotiation seemed overwhelming. . . . But now progress has been made — and already taken for granted. We are engaged in an intense debate on whether we should make changes in Soviet society a precondition for further progress or indeed for following through on commitments already made. . . .

How hard can we press without provoking the Soviet leadership into returning to practices in its foreign policy that increase international tensions? Are we ready to face the crises and increased defense budgets that a return to cold war conditions would spawn?

Is it detente that has prompted repression — or is it detente that has generated the ferment and the demand for openness which we are now witnessing?

For half a century we have objected to Communist efforts to alter the domestic structures of other countries. For a generation of cold war we sought to ease the risks produced by competing ideologies. Are we now to come full circle and insist on domestic compatibility as a condition of progress?

After the collapse of detente, both the U.S. and the U.S.S.R. underwent leadership changes with important implications for Soviet-American relations. U.S. policy under President Ronald Reagan is based on a highly critical view of the Soviet Union. Cooperation with the Soviets has dwindled, and shrill rhetoric from Soviet and American officials has escalated. It is the Reagan administration's policy to improve U.S. national security through a major weapons buildup rather than by stressing arms control. On the Soviet side the deaths of three leaders in as many years have made major policy innovation unlikely. During 1985 the two superpowers sank into a verbal war reminiscent of the cold war of the early 1950s. Soviet propaganda compared Reagan with Hitler, and Reagan described the U.S.S.R. as "an evil empire."

More recently, however, domestic considerations on both sides have led to a slight improvement in relations. On the U.S. side, budget pres-

Seen by some as aggressive and unrealistic, President Reagan's approach to dealing with the Soviet Union is praised by others for its realism and firmness.

Courtesy of Ed Stein.

sures, public fear of nuclear war, public interest in cooperation with the Soviets, and the counsel of some government advisors have pushed the administration to reopen the dialogue with the U.S.S.R. For the Soviets, a much more severe economic crisis and the critical need for domestic reforms have provided the impetus for accommodation. In late 1985 and 1986, after Reagan and Gorbachev met, both sides again began cautiously discussing the possibility of arms control and toned down the violent cold war rhetoric. The Geneva summit raised hopes for improved superpower relations; at Reykjavik expectations for significant arms control agreements first soared and then collapsed.

Complex and fluctuating views have characterized our perceptions of the U.S.S.R. from near the beginning of this century through the present. Although not as dramatic at some times as at others, shifts have been a regular feature of our relationship with the Soviet Union. In the early 1950s the primary Soviet threat was perceived to be Communist subversion, not Soviet military power. Today the threat of nuclear war is clearly predominant.

Echoes from one period are often heard again, many years later. There is therefore continuity, if not consistency, in our relations with the Soviets. The specific details of historical events are easily forgotten, forced from memory by the rush of new issues and concerns; but the lessons we have taught ourselves about the meaning of such distant events linger. They influence our perceptions of the present as well as the future. These lessons, the collective historical memories of Soviets and Americans, are vastly different. And understanding these differences — accepting the immense power of our respective histories — is essential to understanding the other forces that influence U.S.-Soviet perceptions. In the next section we examine one of these forces: the news media.

What specific (and possibly different) historical events have had a significant influence on Soviet and American perceptions?

THE NEWS MEDIA

WORDS AND IMAGES

As American citizens we receive most of our information about the Soviet Union from the news media. This is true for Soviets as well. Newspapers, news magazines, television, or radio news now reach virtually every citizen in the U.S. and U.S.S.R. As a near-constant source of images and information, the media are one of the dominant forces shaping our perceptions today.

Although most of us have never seen Soviet newspapers or newscasts, we still know that the Soviet media are vastly different from that to which we are accustomed. "Propaganda" comes to mind: images of dreary, slogan-filled party newpapers that print lies and conceal the truth in order to brainwash the Soviet people into suspicion and fear of America. The common Soviet view of the American media is similarly harsh: newspapers and television stations controlled by a few wealthy capitalists who put profits before principles and promote distorted, anti-Soviet views.

Contrary to popular perception, complex and diverse Soviet news media present Soviets with a range of information. To be sure, what is reported — and equally important, what is not — is strictly controlled by the state. However, the media in the U.S.S.R. are not completely monolithic. Soviet television offers a surprisingly wide variety of news, entertainment, and educational programming. Children's programming, for example, is regarded as especially good. And criticism, while regulated, does exist in Soviet newspapers.

Even more than Americans, Soviets rely on newspapers as a source of information. Their choices range from the well-known *Pravda* (truth, in English) and *Izvestia* (news), the main papers of the Communist party and Soviet government, to a variety of regional and local newspapers. Some papers focus on industrial or agricultural issues; other publications specialize in sports, film, women, or literature. Some 8,000 dif-

Can one compare the media in the U.S.S.R. to the U.S. media, or is this like comparing apples and oranges?

■ 51

ferent Soviet newspapers publish a total of approximately 170 million copies each year.

The variety of Soviet publications is reminiscent of the diversity of newspapers and magazines available here, but the differences between theirs and ours are great. For example, although major American newspapers may contain 50, 100, or even more pages, the main Soviet newspapers rarely run longer than six pages. Features familiar to Americans, such as travel, horoscopes, and advice to the lovelorn, are generally absent, as is commercial advertising. Home delivery is almost unknown; most Soviet citizens buy their papers at newsstands or read the papers posted daily on public bulletin boards or kiosks. The prices of Soviet newspapers are much lower than their U.S. counterparts. *Pravda*, for example, costs 4 kopeks, roughly a nickel.

But the biggest difference between American and Soviet newpapers is not how much they cost or how much they say, but what they say and how they say it. American papers pride themselves on being objective and try to confine opinion to editorial pages; Soviet newspapers and journalists recognize no such distinction. The "facts" of a newsworthy event are interwoven with the "correct" interpretation. Soviet readers are told not only what happened but also how it fits into the prevailing Marxist-Leninist ideology.

Public postings of newspapers and other announcements serve as a general source of information for many Soviets.

SIPA/Special Features, by Sichou.

The main and explicit function of newspapers in the U.S.S.R. is to contribute to the proper socialization and education of the people. Cases of crime, corruption, and disaster have therefore been traditionally ignored or downplayed by Soviet newspapers. Soviet leaders believe that the lurid headlines and sensationalism of the American press encourage immorality and antisocial behavior. Conveying accurate information, an American journalist's first job, is simply not a top priority of the Soviet press.

The mission of the revolutionary Russian press was articulated by Lenin in his 1902 book, *What Is To Be Done?* An excerpt from that book follows.

The theoreticians write research works. . . . The propagandist does the same thing in the periodical press, and the agitator in public speeches . . . the whole point is that *there is no other way of training* strong political organizations except through the medium of an All-Russian newspaper. . . . For that reason, the principal content of the activity of our Party organization . . . should be work that is both possible and essential in the period of a most powerful outbreak as well as in a period of complete calm, namely, work of political agitation, connected throughout Russia, illuminating all aspects of life, and conducted among the broadest strata of the masses. But this work is *unthinkable* in present-day Russia without an All-Russian newspaper, issued very frequently. . . . A newspaper is not only a collective propagandist and a collective agitator, it is also a collective organizer.

V. I. Lenin, *What Is To Be Done?* (New York: International Publishers, 1969), pp. 67, 157–160.

In contrast with this view of the proper role of the press, the following article, written in 1920 by the preeminent American journalist Walter Lippmann, analyzes U.S. press coverage of the Bolshevik revolution. This classic document illustrates the dramatically different criteria against which the press can be judged. It also demonstrates the capacity of our free press for self-criticism.

It is admitted that a sound public opinion cannot exist without access to the news. There is today a widespread and a growing doubt whether there exists such an access to the news about contentious affairs. This doubt ranges from accusations of unconscious bias to downright charges of corruption, from the belief that the news is colored to a belief that the news is poisoned. On so grave a matter evidence is needed. The study which follows is a piece of evidence. It deals with the reporting of one great event in the recent history of the world. That event is the Russian Revolution from March 1917 to March 1920. The analysis covers thirty-six months and over one thousand is-

Walter Lippmann and Charles Merz, "A Test of the News," *The New Republic,* August 4, 1920.

sues of a daily newspaper. The authors have examined all news items [not editorials] about Russia in that period in the newspaper selected [*The New York Times*]; between three and four thousand items were noted. . . .

The Russian Revolution was selected as the topic, because of its intrinsic importance, and because it has aroused the kind of passion which tests most seriously the objectivity of reporting.

The "whole truth" about Russia is not to be had, and consequently no attempt is made by the authors to contrast the news accounts with any other account which pretends to be the "real truth" or the "true truth." A totally different standard of measurement is used here.

The only question asked is whether the reader of the news was given a picture of various phases of the revolution which survived the test of events, or whether he was misled into believing that the outcome of events would be radically different from the actual outcome. . . .

The news as a whole is dominated by the hopes of the men who composed the news organization. They began as passionate partisans in a great war in which their own country's future was at stake. Until the armistice they were interested in defeating Germany. They hoped until they could hope no longer that Russia would fight. When they saw she could not fight, they worked for [allied] intervention [in Russia] as part of the war against Germany. When the war with Germany was over, the intervention still existed. They found reasons then for continuing the intervention. The German Peril as the reason for intervention ceased with the armistice; the Red Peril almost immediately afterwards supplanted it. The Red Peril in turn gave place to rejoicing over the hopes of the White Generals. When these hopes died, the Red Peril reappeared. In the large, the news about Russia is a case of seeing not what was, but what men wished to see.

This deduction is more important, in the opinion of the authors, than any other. The chief censor and the chief propagandist were hope and fear in the minds of reporters and editors. They wanted to win the war; they wanted to ward off bolshevism. These subjective obstacles to the free pursuit of facts account for the tame submission of enterprising men to the objective censorship and propaganda under which they did their work. For subjective reasons they accepted and believed most of what they were told by the State Department, the so-called Russian Embassy in Washington, the Russian Information Bureau in New York, the Russian Committee in Paris, and the agents and adherents of the old regime all over Europe. For the same reason they endured the attention of officials at crucial points like Helsingors, Omsk, Vladivostok, Stockholm, Copenhagen, London and Paris. For the same reason they accepted reports of governmentally controlled news services abroad, and of correspondents who were unduly intimate with the various secret services and with members of the old Russian nobility.

From the point of professional journalism the reporting of the Russian Revolution is nothing short of a disaster. On the essential questions the net effect was almost always misleading, and misleading news is worse than none at all. Yet on the face of the evidence there is no reason to charge a conspiracy by Americans. They can fairly be charged with boundless credulity, and an untiring readiness to be gulled, and on many occasions with a downright lack of common sense.

Whether they were "giving the public what it wants" or creating a public that took what it got, is beside the point. They were performing the supreme duty in a democracy of supplying the information on which public opinion feeds, and they were derelict in that duty. Their motives may have been excellent. They wanted to save the world. They were baffled by the complexity of affairs, and the obstacles created by war. But whatever the excuses, the apologies, and the extenuation, the fact remains that a great people in a supreme crisis could not secure the minimum of necessary information on a supremely important event. When that truth has burned itself into men's consciousness, they will examine the news in regard to other events, and begin a searching inquiry into the sources of public opinion. That is the indispensible preliminary to a fundamental task of the Twentieth Century: the insurance to a free people of such a supply of news that a free government can be successfully administered.

> **"Soviet readers are told not only what happened but also how it fits into the prevailing Marxist-Lenin ideology."**

The view of the Soviet press articulated by Lenin at the turn of the century was affirmed by Soviet leader Mikhail Gorbachev in his February 1986 speech to the Twenty-Seventh Party Congress. Gorbachev stated that "the Central Committee sees them [the mass media] as an instrument of creation and of expression of the Party's general viewpoint."

Although the functioning of the American press has changed dramatically since the Russian Revolution (the invention of television being one crucial example of the changes), "subjective obstacles to the free pursuit of fact," in Lippmann's words, still exist. What we view as one of the worst aspects of Soviet behavior (tight control of information) often inspires American journalists to commit what the Soviets see as among the most irresponsible acts of our free press.

The Soviet and American concerns were both borne out during the April–May 1986 disaster at the Soviet Chernobyl nuclear reactor complex. As radiation escaped and drifted from the Ukraine into Eastern Europe and Scandanavia, the Soviet silence confirmed the journalistic quip that "a lack of information is almost always followed by poor information." With no official information available, and in keeping with tradition, reporters sought to get the story elsewhere. People who left the Kiev area by train were interviewed; calls were placed to "sources" in the Soviet Union. If more extreme than most, the *New York Post* was not alone in running dramatic and horrifying stories that, at least in the

Although initial Soviet silence about the crisis at the Chernobyl nuclear plant undercut Mikhail Gorbachev's much-proclaimed "new openness" campaign, subsequent reports in the Soviet press were uncharacteristically frank and critical.

Toles, Universal Press Syndicate.

case of the *Post*, are now acknowledged as unsupported and inaccurate. The *Post*'s May 2 story, based on information from the New Jersey *Ukranian Weekly*, reported that "as many as 15,000 people are already dead . . . [and] being buried in a mass grave 150 miles from Chernobyl."

The Soviets were deeply offended by such sensationalist coverage by the American media, even though it resulted largely from their own initial tight-lipped approach to the accident. Moreover — and adding to the dilemma — the Soviet press commonly employs exaggeration and ideological bombast to highlight what it most dislikes about American society. An example of this is the following sarcastic indictment of Michael Jackson.

Al. Naloev, "'Star' Off A Conveyor Belt," *Sovietskaya Kultura* (Soviet Culture), June 14, 1984, p. 7.

However, not even to one mercenary-minded person does this [Michael Jackson's] way of life look great. Its bearers are people of exceptional moral quality. Let's say Michael is a believer, a vegetarian on top of it, doesn't smoke or take drugs. He is sentimental, loves children, and enjoys the movies. Why wouldn't this be an example to follow? And so what if such an idol is totally apolitical? That's a plus, not a minus: only poor blacks and "reds" ever riot. Well-mannered "people of color," recognizing their "primordial masters," serve them with their faith. It wasn't an accident that Jackson had plastic surgery, so much did he want to look 100 percent white, not like a troublemaker, so much did he want to become a full-fledged member of "consumer society," and even more, he wanted to show by his career that the negroes [sic], with their desires and abilities, can be "equal."

That's the rub — why Michael rewards the white establishment. . . .

Many black performers, seduced by the emissaries of show business, went for the remaking of their musical culture. But only one succeeded — Michael Jackson . . . and even though his producer Quincy Jones talked about the return to "African roots," in reality he stood up for a total "leveling" of Michael Jackson's art.

I wanted to know if that was indeed the case. I listened carefully to all nine of his compositions. I remember four: "Billy Jean," "The Girl Is Mine," "Beat It," and the song "Thriller," which doesn't go beyond the boundaries of the already-canonized "new wave." What amazed me was the . . . composer's complete unoriginality . . . characteristic of that ill-famed American lifestyle which the U.S.A. is trying to foist on the rest of the world.

The fundamentally different ideals of the Soviet and American press as described by Lenin and Lippmann — ideological education and accurate information — heavily influence press coverage today. Sometimes the basic differences (which are, paradoxically, easily forgotten because they are so obvious) can lead to disputes over how the American media should cover the U.S.S.R. In early 1986, for example, ABC News allowed a Soviet spokesman, Vladimir Posner, to reply at length to a speech by President Reagan. ABC felt it was in keeping with the requirements of the free American press to allow the expression of alternative viewpoints. The Reagan administration, however, felt that permitting a "trained propagandist" to rebut the president was improper.

The following statements reveal two different perspectives on how the American press should treat Soviet spokespeople such as Vladimir Posner.

Dear Roone:

We were rather astonished last night, following the President's address. . . to see ABC give eight minutes of rebuttal time on national television to a trained propagandist for the Soviet Union.

Mr. Posner performed according to script, disparaging the address as "dishonest," and directly accusing the President of the United States of falsehoods.

Roone, it is our belief that the debate over what America requires — to defend herself, her allies and friends from the awesome military power of the Soviet Union — is a debate for Americans to conduct. Soviet propagandists have no legitimate role in that discussion.

How is a free society's search for consensus served by introducing

Letter from Patrick J. Buchanan, Assistant to the President and Director of Communications, to Roone Arledge, President, ABC News, February 27, 1986.

into its national debate the scripted falsehoods of a regime which has, as its historic and stated purpose, the destruction of that free society? How is the search for truth served by turning ABC's national audience over to an individual whose concept of truth is whatever statement will advance Communist objectives? How is fairness served when the trained propagandist of a hostile regime is put onto the same plane with the President of the United States?

Would you have felt it an expression of objective and balanced journalism, if in the 1930s, Mr. Churchill's calls for the rearmament of *his* country were immediately followed by the BBC's granting of an unrebutted commentary to some functionary for the Third Reich?

By putting Mr. Vladimir Posner on a plane with the President of the United States, . . . ABC gave this Soviet propagandist a standing he does not merit, a legitimacy he does not deserve.

COMPARATIVE COVERAGE

Although comparing current Soviet and American newspaper coverage is inherently a difficult task (for one thing, Soviet papers are much shorter than American papers), Soviet newspapers seem to devote a greater portion of their columns to international affairs than do American papers.

Ellen Mickiewicz, *Media and the Russian Public* (New York: Praeger, 1981), pp. 136–137.

One of the most striking features of the Russian media public is its intense interest in foreign countries and international news events. . . . The thirst for international news cuts across . . . age, sex, and education. . . . [According to a study completed in 1965,] in *Pravda*, about 30 percent of the paper's column inches were devoted to international items. Almost a fifth of [this] space was devoted to stories about the United States, and another quarter of the total foreign news space [was dedicated] to news of NATO and America's European allies. The United States and its allies in Europe were given 44 percent of the international news space, and foreign communist countries only 31 percent.

[By contrast,] an analysis of foreign news information in 1977 in four "elite" American dailies — the *New York Times, Chicago Tribune, Miami Herald,* and *Los Angeles Times* — shows that news about the Soviet Union amounted to roughly 4 percent of all foreign news. News about all communist countries came to 8 percent of all foreign news. Thus the broadcast swath of news about communist countries was not more than 12 percent of foreign news, as compared with the 44 percent of the foreign news in *Pravda* devoted to the United States and its European allies. . . .

We find it difficult to believe that the affiliates of ABC were either aware of — or would have approved of — what was done; and we trust that, in the future, before adopting a posture of benign neutrality as between the crafted words of an American president and the party line of a Soviet functionary, you will give the matter more consideration.

Reluctantly, I tend to agree that Vladimir Posner was allowed too much scope on our program last night. There is nothing wrong with asking a Soviet spokesman for his views of a Presidential speech concerning American posture in relation to the Russians. It is part of what we do. Our production error was in letting him push on at too great a length without an opposing voice to point out the errors and the inconsistencies in what he said.

Complete statement by Richard C. Wald, Senior Vice President, ABC News, February 27, 1986.

Given the vast differences between the roles of the news media here and in the U.S.S.R., one would expect that the American media fosters more accurate perceptions about the Soviet Union than does the Soviet media about the U.S. This is generally correct, but even a free press cannot *guarantee* balanced or complete coverage. Our news media, for example, pays much less attention to the Soviet Union than theirs pays to us. We often ignore important developments in the Soviet Union, and our resulting ignorance has led to misperceptions and fear. The first Soviet explosion of an atomic bomb is a case in point. Given information the U.S. government had, and the Soviets' well-known commitment to keep pace with the U.S., we should not have been surprised that the Soviets developed nuclear weapons four years after we did — but we were. At the policy-making level this is partly attributable to a failure of U.S. intelligence-gathering. Echoed by the news media, this ignorance and shock led to irrational fears of an imminent Soviet attack on or invasion of the U.S.

President Truman's announcement that there has been an atomic explosion in Russia indicates that if the Soviets do not have a successful bomb now they are well on their way toward getting one.

This disturbing probability means that we must assume the worst and make our plans accordingly.

Our most dangerous mistake would be to let ourselves be stampeded into an agreement with Russia on atomic energy controls — an agreement which we could not be sure Russia would keep. . . .

The best way we can discourage Russian aggression is to be too strong to invite attack. To that end we must have more bombs and better bombs than they have. And we must have what it takes to deliver the bombs.

"Russia and the Bomb" *New York World-Telegram*, September 23, 1949.

This is not how we should like to have it. But we must live in that kind of world until all nations are willing to live according to law.

Attention must be given to our defenses, wherever they are weak.

Alaska is vulnerable to air attack. In enemy hands it could be used as a bombing base for operations against the heart of this country.

Alaska is only 56 miles from Russian Siberia. Fairbanks is only 1525 air miles from Seattle, only 2790 air miles from Chicago. From Alaska an enemy could establish advance bases in the Canadian Northwest which would be even nearer our production centers.

Our military posts in Alaska are dangerously undermanned and undersupplied. Housing is inadequate. Storage facilities and utilities are needed. The legislation pending in Congress to remedy these deficiencies should be passed at once so the work can begin on essential construction.

We must not have another Pearl Harbor.

Although the Soviet press is often hostile and unquestioningly critical of American leaders and policies, the following Soviet obituary for President Kennedy expresses warmth and sympathy. Despite the bitter confrontations between Khrushchev and Kennedy over Berlin and the Cuban missile crisis, the broadcast portrays Kennedy in a positive light.

Moscow Radio, November 25, 1963.

Here is a tribute to the memory of President Kennedy written by our observer, Yakov Viktorov: For the American people this has been a day of mourning for President John Kennedy, whose death came so tragically and untimely. The Soviet people and Soviet press share the American people's sorrow at this severe loss. They share the American people's anger and indignation at the criminal activities of the repugnant reactionaries who incited and engineered the brutal assassination of the President.

John Kennedy will go down in history as one of the outstanding U.S. statesmen. In the short period that he held office, he displayed great broadmindedness and a sober appreciation of political realities and of contemporary international development. We remember that in the first days of his tenure in the White House, in his first platform speeches, John Kennedy proclaimed his task to return the United States to the road mapped out by President Franklin Roosevelt, one of the great men to occupy the White House. However, the men who succeeded Roosevelt departed from this road. It is to Kennedy's credit that, despite a certain inconsistency, he did take a sober and rational stand on the main issue of the day, that of war and peace. He recognized in essence the invincibility and vitality of the principle of peaceful coexistence.

Franklin Roosevelt, in his time, always maintained that preserving and consolidating friendship and cooperation between the United States

SEEING BETWEEN THE IMAGES

News from abroad . . . has had a most dramatic impact on [Soviet TV] viewers. It provides a . . . picture to complement and sometimes unintentionally to contradict the mental one burnt into [Soviet] consciousness . . . by the distorting magnifying glass of official rhetoric. After nine or ten segments devoted to familiar subjects, Soviet citizens have a chance "to see" something very different, scenes from beyond their borders. Even if the narrative report that they "hear" accompanying it simply is an echo of the party analysis provided in *Pravda*, Soviet citizens can inspect non-Soviet things and people, visually . . . .

On the surface . . . coverage . . . confirms the general impression of the United States as a land of anti-humanist cowboys shooting up the world for the sake of imperialism, threatening the world with nuclear destruction, exploiting the working class at home, [and] discarding its less fortunates in the dustbins of its inner cities . . . .

However, attentive Soviet viewers get different messages from coverage of the West than those intended. Watching an anti-Star Wars demonstration, a clever viewer concentrates on the clothes worn by demonstrators, the latest fashion in jogging shoes, the household appliances displayed in a store window behind the scene or the cars whizzing by the protesters. The ordinary details of daily life become the extraordinary elements in video landscapes that attract attention. Constantly subjected to the echo chamber in which propagandistic ideas reverberate ceaselessly, viewers become inured to such messages. Their eyes "read between the lines" of the purposeful video text.

"Seeing Between the Images," Jonathan Sanders, Director and Founder of the Working Group on Soviet Television, Harriman Institute, Columbia University.

and the U.S.S.R. was an immutable prerequisite for building peace. John Kennedy also realized the full significance and necessity of bettering and strengthening Soviet-U.S. relations in the spirit of businesslike cooperation for the good of the people of both countries and the cause of general peace. Both Roosevelt and Kennedy shared an understanding of the new factors in the history of mankind which have taken such a forceful grip on life and which have radically altered the balance of power in the world arena. Further [sic] historians, in analyzing the development of American policy, will undoubtedly trace the line from Franklin Roosevelt to John Kennedy. They will link Kennedy's name with U.S. participation in the history-making Moscow test-ban treaty, which was concluded at the Soviet Union's initiative.

It must also be noted that when it came to domestic policy, John Kennedy did not take the road of his immediate predecessors. He strongly opposed the sway of racism, which he called "a blight on America." The course steered by President Kennedy in search of a peaceful settlement of controversial international issues and his speeches flaying racism aroused anger and hatred against him among the wild men, among the rabid reactionaries who, as the tragic march of events has shown, even stooped to a horrible crime: to remove Kennedy from the political arena.

Let us ask: Who profited from the assassination of Kennedy? The answer makes it clear that we are dealing with a criminal conspiracy spun by the darkest forces of reaction. The champions of the cold war, together with the wild men of all and every ilk, saw and realized perfectly well that every one of the President's measures aimed at international relaxation met with enthusiastic approval of the majority of the American people. This is indicated most convincingly by the way public opinion in the United States reacted to the signing of the Moscow treaty. It should not be forgotten that the election campaign has begun in the United States, and the election struggle is most acute this year. The enemies of President Kennedy and his administration's policy could not but understand that their fight against Kennedy's candidacy was hopeless in view of his popularity and growing prestige, so they killed the President. Now the reactionaries are mobilizing all their forces and means to remove all traces of their horrible crime, but we are certain justice will triumph and the assassins will be found.

Today, the day of President Kennedy's funeral, the Soviet people, together with all people of good will, extend their condolences to the people of the United States. Premier Khrushchev wrote to President Lyndon Johnson that the Soviet Government and the Soviet people share the American people's grief at so great a loss and they express the hope that the search for solutions of controversial issues, to which President Kennedy contributed so substantially, will be continued in the interests of peace and for the good of all mankind. The best way to keep alive the memory of President Kennedy, whose death was so untimely, is by continuing his lofty initiative permeated by a striving to rid the world of the menace of a thermonuclear war.

> **"The understanding or perception of an event depends on the perspective from which that event is viewed."**

Perhaps the most interesting way to compare the American and Soviet press is to look at how each side portrays the same event. The following reprints illustrate how *Pravda* and American newspapers covered two stories.

"Marcos Quits Presidency, Leaves Manila in U.S. Helicopter; Aquino Sworn In; U.S. Recognizes New Government," *The Current Digest of the Soviet Press*, vol. XXXVII, no. 9 (February 26, 1986).

The Philippines: Changing of the Guard" (*Pravda*, February 26, 1986, p. 12); *Manila, February 25 (Tass)* — Philippine President F. Marcos has resigned his powers as head of state; he left the presidential palace in a helicopter. It is reported that he and his family were taken to Clark Field, the American air base; from there they will be flown to a "third country."

C. Aquino, sworn in today as President of the country, announced the formation of a provisional government. . . .

The personnel of American bases in the Philippines have been placed in a state of heightened combat readiness in case "defense of military facilities" becomes necessary. U.S. Navy units, including the flagship Blue Ridge and the attack carrier Enterprise, have been stationed off the shores of the Philippine archipelago. In case "extreme circumstances" should arise, units of Marines and instructors in conducting punitive operations against a civilian population have been transferred from Okinawa.

If Soviet and American media cover the same news events and portray them differently, how does this affect Soviet and American thinking about what happens in the world?

Manila — Twenty years of often-tyrannical rule ended Tuesday night in an explosion of street celebrations as President Ferdinand E. Marcos abandoned the presidency of the Philippines and fled the country in a U.S. Air Force jet.

Marcos' departure climaxed a crisis that began with a flawed and fraudulent presidential election and ended with both his army and his people rising up against him in combined revolt.

Three hours after U.S. helicopters had carried Marcos, his family and close associates from Malacanang Palace, U.S. Secretary of State George P. Shultz announced U.S. recognition of the new government headed by Corazon Aquino.

Although Shultz said the United States had offered asylum to Marcos, his family and a handful of close aides, it was not yet clear Tuesday where the deposed president would take up residence. After spending the night at the sprawling Clark Air Base, 50 miles northwest of the capital, his party was flown to the U.S. Pacific island territory of Guam. There were reports that it would proceed to Honolulu later.

Mark Fineman and Nick B. Williams, Jr., "Marcos Quits; Crowds Rejoice, American Asylum Offered to Ex-Philippine Ruler," *Los Angeles Times,* February 26, 1986.

Protest to the U.S. State Department (*Pravda*, August 23, 1985, p. 5) — In connection with the allegations, spread by the U.S. State Department, about the use in the Soviet Union of "chemical substances for surveillance of staff members of the U.S. Embassy," the U.S.S.R. Embassy in Washington has stated the following to the State Department:

"The Soviet side resolutely denies the absurd fabrications alleging that some kind of chemical substances are used with respect to the personnel of U.S. institutions in the U.S.S.R. We have never done, and are not now doing, anything of the kind. Attempts to make such claims against us are not only completely inappropriate but also absolutely unacceptable.

"One cannot help seeing behind the raising of this farfetched question a quite definite scheme — to prepare the ground for another slander campaign against the Soviet Union, poison the atmosphere in relations between our countries, and stir up enmity toward Soviet people.

"Moscow Denies Use of Chemicals for Surveillance of U.S. Embassy Personnel, Charges Slander Campaign Against U.S.S.R.," *The Current Digest of the Soviet Press*, vol. XXXVII, no. 34 (September 18, 1985).

"It is outrageous that the American side has deemed it possible to resort to such a gross falsehood, the goals of which are far from the interests of improving our relations.

"In lodging a protest with respect to the provocative action taken against the U.S.S.R. we warn that the American side will bear full responsibility for the possible consequences of actions of this sort."

Niles Lathem, "U.S. to Sovs: Clean Up Act on 'Killer Spy Dust,'" *Boston Herald*, August 23, 1985.

Los Angeles — The White House yesterday blasted the Soviet Union for stonewalling on the issue of planting potentially cancer-causing chemical dust on American diplomats in Moscow. . . .

"Our first objective in this case is to stop the Soviets from using the chemical against our personnel, and we expect this will occur," [White House spokesman] Speakes said.

But, holding out an olive branch, Speakes added that he does not believe this case will affect Reagan's plans to hold a summit meeting with Soviet leader Mikhail Gorbachev this November.

"We intend to proceed with the meeting," said Speakes. . . .

Speakes' comment came as White House officials privately revealed that the use of spy dust is not the first instance of dirty tricks employed by the KGB to keep track of U.S. diplomats.

The most famous case of KGB mischief-making was in the early 1950s, when the Soviets placed a listening device in a replica of the great seal of the United States that hung in the U.S. embassy in Moscow.

The KGB . . . also has bombarded the U.S. embassy with microwaves in an effort to activate listening devices or jam U.S. communications equipment.

Last March the Soviets also were accused of placing sensitive sonar devices in the walls of the U.S. embassy, giving them the capability of picking up what was written on U.S. embassy typewriters.

Why do we believe either the Soviet or the American press explanations of the so-called spy dust incident?

Another obstacle to accurate portrayal of the U.S. and U.S.S.R. in each country's news media could be called the problem of perspective. The understanding or perception of an event depends on the perspective from which that event is viewed. A case in point is the Soviet Union's 1983 downing of Korean Air Lines flight 007. To the U.S. this was a brutal, premeditated act of murder. The Soviets justified it as an act of caution and self-defense against what was believed to be a U.S. spy plane. The U.S. would not shoot down a civilian aircraft under such circumstances; the fact that the Soviets did tells a great deal about the Soviet fear of intruders across their borders, especially over top-secret military bases and testing ranges.

Comparing American media coverage of the KAL 007 incident with that of an incident in February 1973, when the Israelis shot down an Arab civilian jetliner, reveals certain underlying perceptions, even expectations. The facts in both cases were unclear at the time of the inci-

ALBATROSS

The Soviet shooting of KAL 007 outraged the world and was seen by many as further evidence of Soviet belligerence and paranoia.

From *Herblock Through the Looking Glass* (W. W. Norton, 1984).

dents. Confronted with confusion, many press organizations made assumptions about Israeli and Soviet motivations. In both cases, the assumptions were in keeping with commonly held perceptions about U.S. allies and adversaries. For many reasons we may never know the full story of KAL 007, and there are obvious and vast differences between Israel and the Soviet Union. But the manner in which the press covered these two events is noteworthy.

THE NEWS
MEDIA

"Murder in the Air: Deadly Decision Mirrors Soviet State," editorial, *The Clarion-Ledger*, Jackson, MS, September 2, 1983.

The shooting down of a commercial airliner by a Soviet warplane is an act of barbarism singular in its savagery for international behavior.

The full story will never be known. But it is increasingly clear that the Soviets deliberately decided to shoot down an unarmed plane because it had entered Soviet airspace, and that it mattered not at all if it cost innocent lives. Apparently in this case, 269 lives, including that of Georgia congressman Larry McDonald.

It is unclear what responses can be made that can go beyond the contempt and anger that the civilized world now expresses. In an age living within a push-button of annihilation, the options are limited.

But it surely must prompt millions of people to again examine the basic nature of the Soviet state. That state — history's most colossal failure — is a power only because of its bullying capacity for nuclear holocaust.

Since Leonid Brezhnev's death the public has been gulled by perceptions of a potentially more conciliatory Soviet Union. The horror in Afghanistan is halfway around the world, peace would have a chance if only the West disarmed, everyone — *everyone* — shares this same longing for no nukes and brotherhood.

The reality is something else. Yuri Andropov may not have ordered his pilots to shoot down an unarmed plane, but someone did. And it was someone, we suspect, in reasonably high military or political authority, in a position responsible enough to reflect the attitude of a significant segment of Soviet officialdom.

It is a blood-curdling thought that such minds are also within reach of the nuclear button. That the Soviets acted to hide what might not be known to Western intelligence is a possibility of equally fearful ramifications.

There has to be a means of living with international murderers in view of the alternative. This argues against the more drastic responses, especially as the Soviets — clearly on the defensive now in world forums — have a tendency to react elsewhere. But it does argue for a reawakening to the truth, that the Soviets' system is monstrous, that they have a capacity for striking against the innocent with deadly precision, and that only the armed strength of their opponents has maintained civilization and world peace.

This truth won't bring back the dead, but it can well save the rest of us.

"Rule of Reason, Guide to Peace," editorial, *The Plain Dealer*, Cleveland, OH, February 23, 1973.

The tragic crash landing of the Libyan airliner in the Sinai Desert illustrates that sound judgment is as necessary as good will in keeping the peace in areas of high tension and bitter feeling.

What degree of force may a country use to compel an air pilot to land his craft when the airplane is flying over forbidden territory without permission? Experts in international law seem to agree there are no clearly established principles.

But there is a basic rule which makes good sense, the rule of reason. So states Louis Sohn, professor of international law at Harvard University. "On one hand," he says, "a country has the right to protect its interests. On the other hand, the aim should be to avoid jeopardizing lives. The big issue is fact. To what extent were warnings given and did the pilot refuse to obey?"

Israeli officials maintain the French pilot of the Libyan liner refused to heed orders to land after flying over Israeli military installations along the Suez Canal. So Israeli fighter planes fired on the big passenger plane.

Egyptian sources claim the pilot lost his course in a storm, was unaware he was over hostile territory and might have thought the Israeli fighter planes were friendly Egyptian MIGs.

In such a situation, says Prof. Andreas Lowenfeld of New York University, the guiding legal principle would be that a nation (Israel here) should exercise its protective right "with a minimum of force."

Investigations have been called for but, on the face of things, any testimony will be emotional and the absolute truth will be elusive. This much is certain, however. The "rule of reason" did not prevail and sound judgment was not exercised. The death list is testimony to that.

Although reports from the print media certainly influence our perceptions, television seems to do so to an even greater extent. By the end of the 1950s TV replaced newspapers and magazines as Americans' primary source of news and information. In the Soviet Union the same revolution took place 15 years later, and today there are some 65 million television sets in the U.S.S.R. Nationwide, over 86 percent of the Soviet people have access to a television. In urban areas, about 90 percent of families own their own sets. These figures still lag somewhat behind those for the U.S., but they represent a tremendous leap for a society in which the media play such an important role.

In addition to television programs and newspaper stories, radio broadcasts are a primary source of information for Soviets, particularly those living in rural areas. Many Soviet listeners also tune in to foreign radio stations — such as the BBC and the Voice of America — to supplement domestic broadcasts. By some estimates, as many as 37 percent of Soviet adults listen to foreign radio, giving such broadcasts a significant role in the shaping of Soviet perceptions about the rest of the world.

But as access to and ownership of TV sets continues to grow, television may yet come to dominate the Soviet media as thoroughly as it does those of the U.S. And as the medium has expanded, it has also grown in sophistication. Although many Soviet TV programs appear dreary and propagandistic to Americans, others are remarkably lively and modern. "Rural Hour," a boring show about agricultural production and events on the collective farm, is one of the least watched by Soviet viewers. "Rhythmic Gymnastics," a flashy aerobics exercise program featuring shapely women working out to the pulsating beat of loud rock music, has a remarkably Western style. Soviet television also features excellent coverage of sports events and a wide range of educational programs.

One major difference between Soviet and American television is the number of channels. Even in Moscow, only two national channels broadcast throughout the day. In addition, an educational channel comes on the air at 4:00 in the afternoon, and a local Moscow channel begins at 7:00 pm. Another major difference between Soviet and American television is the role of commercials and advertising. Commercials, "reklami," appear infrequently on Soviet television. When they do, they are bunched in groups for five or ten minutes. Many of them are actually public service announcements concerning health or safety. Others advertise radios, televisions, and other products of the state-run Soviet industries.

"Vremya," which translates as "Time," is the daily national news program of the Soviet Union. Broadcast every night at 9:00 p.m., it reaches approximately 150 million viewers. The news, which lasts from one-half to a full hour, is divided into several segments. Government news begins the program, followed by domestic and regional events. International news follows, and "Vremya" concludes with sports and weather.

As with Soviet newspapers, television in the U.S.S.R. is carefully designed to cultivate "proper" values in its viewers. The U.S. is generally cast in a negative light, and news about accidents, disasters, and crime in the Soviet Union is usually absent. Even television game shows convey a particular message. The competition is friendly and the subjects are educational, designed to popularize various occupations and encourage positive values. Prizes are small and everybody usually wins something. With the exception of war films, Soviet television offers little of the violence to which American viewers are accustomed.

What follows is a translated listing of a typical day's TV programming in Moscow. One obvious difference is that there is no programming from approximately midnight (24.00) until 8:00 a.m.

	Channel 1	Channel 2	Moscow Channel
8.00	"Time" (news)	Gymnastics	
8.20		"It's All the Same," artistic film	
8.40	Rhythmic Gymnastics		
9.10	Young Pioneers, film journal		
9.20	Sports Lottery		
9.30	"Alarm Clock"		

	Channel 1	Channel 2	Moscow Channel
9.50		Mommy's School	
10.00	"I Serve the USSR!"		
10.20		Program from Armenian TV	
11.00	Morning Mail		
11.30	Travelers' Club		
11.35		Russian Word	
12.05		"And That's All There Is on That," artistic TV film, part 6	
12.30	"Musical Kiosk"		
13.00	Rural Hour		
13.15		TV Bridge: Moscow-Washington, "On Progress of Soviet and American Scientists in the Field of Cardiology"	
14.00	Multiplication		
14.20	Film Sketches of Australia		
14.45	"Reader's Club"		
15.15		In the Animal World	
15.35	V. Vasilev plays piano		
15.55	Encounters on Soviet Soil		
16.10	Visiting the Fairy Tales: "The Snow Maiden," artistic film		
16.15		Our Correspondents Speak	

	Channel 1	Channel 2	Moscow Channel
16.45		International fencing competition, "Moscow Saber"	
17.15		Two concerts by G. Teleman	
17.45		Hockey: "Falcon" vs. Central Army Club, 2nd and 3rd periods	
18.00	International Panorama		
18.45	Film Posters		
19.00			"Blue Roses for Ballerinas," film concert
19.15		Advertisements	
19.20		"Inspiration," documentary TV movie	
19.30		Young People and the World	
19.45	Final concert from "Songs of 1985," recorded December 29		Advertisements
20.00		Good Night, Kids!	Good Night, Kids!
20.15		European men's skating championships	Popular science films
20.45			Information Bureau
21.00	"Time" (news)	"Time"	"Time"
21.45	"Songs of 1985" repeat	"Together Again," movie	Hockey: "Spartacus" vs. "Chemist," 2nd and 3rd periods
22.55			Moscow News
23.20	News		

Aside from the problems of bias and perspective, which exist to varying degrees in both the American and Soviet media, there is another obstacle that only the U.S. media face in their reporting on the U.S.S.R. This is the problem of access. Soviet journalists have relatively free access to a wealth of information — published and personal — about the U.S., but American journalists' access to information in the U.S.S.R. is severely restricted. The following article describes what it is like for U.S. correspondents in Moscow.

Joseph Finder, "Reporting from Russia," *Washington Journalism Review*, June 1985.

The Moscow beat is variously a sought-after and an undesirable assignment in journalism. In television journalism it is, with some exceptions, considered a detour on the way up the ladder, a subject of dramatization (Clark Gable, playing a Moscow correspondent in the 1940 movie "Comrade X," utters the memorable line, "Face the facts, baby. There ain't no news in Russia"). . . . In a world of expanding telecommunications, what purpose is now served by reporters in the Land of No News?

Seymour Topping, managing editor of the *New York Times* and a former Moscow correspondent, gives a complex and surprising answer to this question. Most information, he says, cannot be contained in the Soviet Union; it will always get out one way or another. "But the subtle distinction about being able to write a story in Moscow," he says, "is that the story has authority. Let us say there is a political telegram from the embassy in Moscow that goes to someone on the State Department Soviet desk, where it's made public. That information has gone through the spectrum of information of the mind of that person in the State Department. Very often there's a difference in interpretation of information between the reporting officer in Moscow and the State Department or intelligence people in Washington who are receiving that information. There's an intermediate mind. Reporters here get it once removed; here, it is made to fit into policy enunciated in Washington.". . .

Of the 24 American reporters in Moscow, the one with probably the best connections to apparatchiks of the Soviet government is the *Washington Post*'s Dusko Doder, who [has recently returned] to Washington after a four-year assignment in the Soviet Union. I interviewed Doder . . . in the *Post*'s office . . . at 7/4 Kutuzovsky Prospekt, which also houses the Associated Press, United Press International, *Newsweek* and the *Chicago Tribune*. It is a complex of singularly unattractive ecru brick buildings known to its inhabitants as the "foreigners' ghetto." When I arrived early one evening — American reporters in Moscow get to the office late in the day and work until midnight or later, because of the time difference between Moscow and home — Doder was busy typing out a story on a large wooden teletype terminal. I waited in the bureau's other room, which was lined with reference books from the *Great Soviet Encyclopedia* to scholarly works on the Soviet government and deco-

"This is the best post in the world . . . and in an odd sense it's the freest."
American journalist in Moscow

rated with charts of the Soviet leaders. Photographs of those deceased or removed from power were marked with black X's.

Doder, an animated though somewhat weary-looking man with deep-set dark eyes, appeared, announced that he had just sent off a story on talks between the Soviet Union and China, and offered me a cup of instant coffee. I asked him how he had obtained the information for the article. "I talked to some of the Chinese I know," he said. "Some of them I've known for quite a while, and I can tell when they're not being straight with me. It helps to have been here for a while. This is my second tour of duty — I was here for the United Press in the early '70s."

I remarked that one must get tired, after a while, of the frustrations of working in Moscow. "Oh, everyone's got stories about harassment," he said dismissively. "Once in a while, sure, they harass us. They'll cut off the phone, although always for a short time. You'll have an unpleasant exchange with some low-level official, and then the phone goes dead. The phone is a vital instrument here, without it we're completely isolated. They don't censor us, haven't for years, but every so often I'll be typing out a story and the teletype is *interrupted*. Just for a minute. Probably some flunky reads what's going over the wire and doesn't like it, and *wham*. But these are rare instances. What gets to you are the everyday hassles of life. This morning I took my son to the airport, and the customs inspector told him to open everything. He said to me, 'You could be smuggling something out through him,' I told the guy.' 'First of all, I don't need to do that, and you know it. And how stupid do you think I am? Would you put *your* son in danger that way?' The guy didn't answer."

I asked Doder why foreign reporters are all sequestered in separate housing. "I'm convinced the reason they coop us up in the foreigners' ghetto is only 50 percent for security reasons, to watch us," he said. "The other 50 percent is to keep us from seeing how sad life is here. They're terribly concerned about what America thinks. They don't want us to get robbed or to see people standing in line. But out *there* is the real story — what the trends are, what the mood is, whether life is getting better or worse."

"Is it important to know Russian?"

"Knowing Russian frees you from dependence on the diplomats and the other correspondents. But it's not everything. . . . There have been some people whose knowledge of Russian is fantastic, and they could be here for 50 years and not have a clue how this place works."

"But does that make a difference?"

He picked up a cigar stub from an ashtray and lighted it. "If you want to write about this place accurately it does. Let's face it, Americans really aren't interested in Russia. They think of Russia as a military power and not much else. The average guy just wants to hear how bad it is; that makes him feel good. It's the negative stories that get the front-page play. It's easy to succumb to that temptation, but I don't think I do."

The *Washington Post*, I said, had a reputation since the Watergate days of being a heavily "investigative" newspaper, and I wondered whether its editors expected a similar treatment in Moscow. "A lot of us are used to being hard-nosed and adversarial," he said, and lighted the cigar butt again. "Here, however, one runs the risk of taking that negative attitude too far. If you're looking for something to complain about, you'll find an abundance. This is the best post in the world — it's the most important and in an odd sense it's the freest, because you can write whatever you want and no one can check up on you — but life here can be lousy. It can easily get to you, and it's easier to write when you're mad. Your adrenalin starts pumping, the words flow, and then there's the fact that you instinctively know a negative story is news. I'm glad I wasn't here during the Korean Air Lines crisis. I was in Washington, thank God. There was such hysteria in the U.S., and I know I would have been expected to fulfill Americans' expectations. I was having lunch with Henry Kissinger not long after and he asked, 'Dusko, why didn't they immediately say it was a spy plane and convene an emergency session of the U.S. [sic] Security Council, and thereby put us on the defensive — force us to prove it was *not* spy plane?' Well, you can see Henry's brilliant mind at work there. I said, 'Henry, you don't understand their mentality. They could have done that but they waited. They didn't know what sort of evidence we had; they weren't sure we had tapes of the pilots' conversations.' At times like that they're extremely cautious. . . ."

Perceptions, symbols and interpretations seemed to remain on Doder's mind. . . . "This is an ecclesiastical society, even Talmudic in a sense. The written word is all-important. Nobody speaks impromptu. Speeches are read from prepared texts. When you read a paper here, the language is repetitive and carefully chosen. Suddenly something will be phrased ever so slightly differently, and you must ask why. Is it a signal? Knowledge is power, and so information here is scarce, meted out on a 'need-to-know' basis from the top down. They make it as hard for us reporters as possible. Much of the important news is held until the evening news show, "Vremya," at 9 o'clock at night. All of the government bureaus are closed then; it's impossible for us to get any further information. This is partly by design, I think." He continued, "In the old days, during the censorship, the trick was in getting information out past the censor. Now, you can get anything out, and what is important is how you say it, what interpretation you give the information you have."

I asked him what there is of value to report in Moscow that cannot be taken from a Tass teletype in Washington. "We don't report," he said. "There's nothing to report here. We analyze. Everything we do is analysis; everything else is worthless. That's why I'm amused by all the American Sovietologists who presume to know what Russia's all about when some of them have never even set foot here. There's some notion that *Russia* is synonymous with the *government*, and while the government is no doubt extremely important, the two aren't synonymous. You can't understand the nature of this place, the evolution of the society, the

Do our perceptions of the U.S.S.R. change when new reporters go to Moscow?

political culture from which the leaders come, without being here. Could you understand America without ever visiting it? The idea is ridiculous."

I asked Bob Zelnick, then ABC's Moscow correspondent and now its correspondent in Tel Aviv, . . . if . . . film was ever censored. "I wouldn't say they *never* would," Zelnick said. "They *haven't*. They just don't do that. If they don't like a story we're doing they don't let us put it on the 'bird,' the satellite, which they operate. They used to say, if they didn't like what I was working on, that the satellite was *na remont* — being repaired. Now they know us better, and when I call and tell them I'm doing a story on, say, the Soviet military, they just say, 'I can't help you with that.' So we put it on a plane to Frankfurt or London and beam it to New York the next day. That's usually no big deal. If I'm working on something on the Soviet military buildup it's not something that's got to be done on a deadline. . . ."

I mentioned to Zelnick that one of his predecessors as ABC's Moscow correspondent, Anne Garrels, had once compared raising a camera in the Soviet Union to raising an M-16 — everybody scatters. Zelnick said it was not, in his experience, quite that bad, but then added that two weeks before, he had been taken away in a paddy wagon by the Soviet police for interviewing a few Soviet peace activists on film. He showed me, in a small production room crowded with electronic arcana, the rough cuts of this story, which was broadcast on March 16, 1984. . . . A policeman in an olive drab uniform with epaulets suddenly appears and says brusquely, in Russian, "Goodbye! Turn that off." He waves them away. In the next clip, the woman is being interviewed again, at another location nearby, and the same policeman appears. . . . He stands squarely before the camera and puts his hand up to its lens. "Come with me. Turn that off."

Zelnick, who was watching with me, said, "Gary, our cameraman, left the camera on. These guys don't know how American television cameras work."

The footage now continues inside a Soviet paddy wagon, which is mostly dark except for light coming through bars on the window. "Good shot, huh?" Zelnick said. The completed story was remarkable because the shots of the policeman's interruption and of the inside of a paddy wagon conveyed vividly Soviet sensitivity about the peace group in a way that mere words could not. . . .

The *New York Times* bureau . . . is by far the most spacious of the foreign news offices I visited. Serge Schmemann (his last name is Russian, his first French) is one of two reporters for the *Times* in the Moscow bureau. . . .

I asked [Schmemann] what can be learned in Moscow that can't be learned in Washington. "In Washington you can't go out into the street and find out that people *favored* what Andropov was doing. You meet people; you talk with people in the subway. I don't mean 'man-on-the-street' interviews. I mean contacts with people. Sometimes I'll go to a beer bar and stand around sipping a beer. Of course, you've got to be careful. An American correspondent is a combination of everything that is evil. The Soviet press denounces us as spies, as betrayers of the motherland. Drop the fact too soon that you're a correspondent and you'll send them running.

"Let's take the K.A.L. incident — that said a lot about how this place functions. You heard all that talk about 'sacred borders.' They know all that in Washington. But we're here to explore why. It took the Soviet government *five days* to admit it shot down the plane. But why? You remember one of the first things to come out was that interview on Soviet television with the pilot who said that he saw the plane entering Soviet airspace and *he thought of his family asleep below?* Well, that had

SELF-CRITICISM

Since the accession of Gorbachev there has been a remarkably open debate in the Soviet Union over the performance of the Soviet media — in this case, some frank criticism of their television coverage of the West.

I t is difficult today to imagine television without news broadcasts, particularly the most popular of them — the "Vremya" program. It is one of the main themes of satisfying Soviet viewers' needs for information and has established a firm psychological propensity for television news. . . .

Pravda readers write that they still encounter [in television news] superficial subject matter and eulogizing and that some interviews and reports seem to be rehearsed and slick. Sometimes journalists do not examine the essence of events and viewers learn about them only some time later. . . .

Particular attention has repeatedly been drawn to the improvement of international news reporting and to the need for a rapid response to and more thorough analysis of world events. Judging by letters to *Pravda* and

opinion polls, viewers expect more than they are currently getting from "Vremya" in this respect. Coverage of the capitalist world is monotonous. Programs primarily show rallies, demonstrations, and protests. They rarely describe scientific or technological achievements or what the latter mean for ordinary workers under capitalist conditions. . . .

There are also "blank areas" in the international news coverage. I refuse to believe that the coverage of life abroad is limited to showing a street where our correspondents stand against a background of speeding limousines and eye-catching store displays and advertisements and comment on items in the local press. Furthermore, the film sequences on such topics do not always match the content of the reports.

Dimitri Lyubotsvetov, "Time on the Screen: Remarks on Television News," *Pravda*, May 19, 1986, p. 3 (translated by *Pravda Pulse*, Fort Pierce, FL).

a powerful effect. Then at last they said they had fired at the plane. I talked to Russians here after that announcement, and they said, 'Of course!'" He slammed his fist on the desk, deepened his voice, and assumed a Russian accent. "'What do you think? Of *course* we did it! What the hell was that plane up there for?' They broke the news bit by bit in order to prepare the people here, and it was done quite effectively. That's the sort of thing you can only see here."

What about dissidents? Critics of American coverage of the Soviet Union have long maintained that American correspondents tend to exaggerate the importance of dissidents.

When I asked Nick Daniloff, of *U.S. News & World Report*, about the coverage of dissidents and how he dealt with this problem he told me, "I don't consort with dissidents. The magazine considers them a passing phenomenon of little interest. In a political sense they don't have an influence — and they are perishing." I suggested to Schmemann that this must be an ongoing problem for a reporter for the *Times*, a paper so well known in the Soviet Union. "Ah, yes, dissidents," he said. "This is always a problem, both in whether to see them and whether to run their story. In some ways it's a humanitarian dilemma. How do I tell them, 'You are of no interest'? Do I meet with them? 'Your wife is on a hunger strike' — how do I tell them to go to hell?"

He reached over to a desk drawer, unlocked it, and pulled out a folder thick with letters typed in Russian on onionskin. "Look at this. It's heart-rending. In the 1970s, the dissident movement was fairly unified; it was a time when groups tended to help one another. They've managed to crush this. Now you have thousands of separate people, working separately — people who have infinite faith in America. They believe if they can just get their story to *America* their problems are solved." He gestured with the back of his hand at his brown, rotary-dial American telephone and said ironically, "You see, I usually speak to the dissidents. Other reporters do me the disservice, if they're busy, of shoving them off on me."

I asked Schmemann whether working in the Soviet Union is especially frustrating.

"Functioning in a police state is not very easy. But, oddly, life here is *intensified* by the system. Every reporter who leaves here misses the place tremendously. Nowhere else do you have these all-night discussions in the kitchen on What Is Truth. Still, the obstacles can drive you crazy. There are Soviet officials I talked to all the time when they were at the United Nations and I was covering the U.N. who have been transferred here and now won't even see me. When we get outside of Moscow we usually have somewhat better access. Then again, you can get stonewalled so royally you sit there steaming. When I was in Siberia I met with the first secretary of the Party in a small town. I said to her, 'Name one major problem you have,' and she replied, after thinking a bit, 'Maybe our only problem is that we *try too hard.*' Nevertheless, I think travel is a critical aspect of covering the Soviet Union. Your juices start flowing again. I get so used to life in Moscow that I won't even notice the propaganda slogans across the street. Moscow is the center of a major empire. It's got its own tempo. It's different from the rest of the country. You begin to forget this place is atypical."

Given these obstacles, just how well does the American media cover events in the Soviet Union? How successful are today's correspondents in overcoming certain American biases and misperceptions about the U.S.S.R.? The following exchange between Stephen Cohen, an American specialist on the U.S.S.R., and Robert Gillette, a former Moscow correspondent for the *Los Angeles Times*, offers two conflicting answers on this question.

In recent years the quality of American newspaper coverage of the Soviet Union has been as bad as I can remember. Too much of it is one-dimensional, distorted, and factually wrong.

Here, I think, is the prevailing image of the Soviet Union that emerges nowadays in the American media: It's a crisis-ridden, decaying system composed of a stagnant, inefficient economy; corrupt

Stephen F. Cohen, "Soviet State and Society as Reflected in the American Media," *Nieman Reports* (Cambridge, MA), Winter 1984.

bureaucratic elite; a sick, cynical, and restive society; and an aging, inept political leadership than cannot change or make policy, only manipulate it.

Part of this picture is true, but on the whole, it is a crudely distorted caricature without context, without complex realities, without balance. It reminds me of those well-known Soviet press descriptions of American life based solely on accounts of unemployment, drug addiction, street crime, and political corruption. But it is this generally distorted American media image that contributes greatly to the plethora of misleading news stories and commentary on specific Soviet developments. . . . Most American media coverage of the Soviet Union focuses on one of three aspects of the system: Soviet leaders, or what I call media leaderology; Soviet policy and policy-making; and relations between the Soviet party-state and the society below.

Let me start with leaders and media leaderology. American coverge of Soviet leaders has been intense since Brezhnev's death in November 1982, because there's been a constant process of leadership succession ever since. That coverage has been very bad — uninformed, wildly speculative, and unself-critically contradictive. . . .

My point is not that you people guessed wrong about the next Soviet leader; so did many Sovietologists. My point is that media coverage of Soviet leaders lacks any sense of the actual leadership system that has evolved over the last three decades. It's a system of balances and checks on personal power. It's a system where several institutions and political bosses, in and outside of the Politburo, play crucial roles. It's a system in which many powerful groups seem not to want a truly strong leader. And it's a system where a top leader needs several years — at least five — to consolidate any real power. If American journalists had noted any of these important features of the Soviet leadership system, they could not possibly have written or broadcast much of what has appeared in the last two or three years.

Let me give you a recent example. Last week NBC News did a television story from Moscow on Chernenko's alleged successors. It presented as the leading candidates Gorbachev, Romanov, Gromyko, Ustinov, Aliev, and Tikhonov. Only two of the six actually sit on both the Politburo and the Secretariat, which is a prerequisite for becoming General Secretary. Incidentally, the chances of Aliev becoming General Secretary are probably less that Jesse Jackson's chances of becoming president of the United States. He isn't a Russian, or even a Slav.

Media coverage of Soviet policy, foreign and domestic, has not been much better. Virtually all commentary on the possibility of change in foreign policy is tied to the alleged personal quirks or personalities of this or that Soviet leader. You will recall, for example, the media's brief fixation with Andropov's alleged closet Westernism and liberalism. . . . I would be among the last to minimize the role of personality in political leadership. But this kind of media analysis trivializes the policy-making

process in the Soviet Union. What the media fails to understand is that a real policy-making process exists in the Soviet Union, and that it is much larger than any one Politburo leader. In recent years, that policy-making process has come to involve hundreds, and maybe even thousands, of high Soviet officials — an entire political or policy class, to which the supreme leadership, the Politburo, is beholden. And within that policy class, there exist many different groups, vested interests, perspectives, and even different Soviet ideologies. That is, within that policy class, there exist long-standing, deep-rooted, fundamental conflicts over policy. . . .

Policy toward the United States has been the subject of fierce controversy inside Soviet policy circles for many years, a hotly disputed issue between advocates of detente and proponents of Cold War. The dramatic upsurge of cold war attitudes in Moscow today, which some of you have reported, isn't simply manipulated. It reflects an important upsurge in the political fortunes of the Soviet cold war lobby, and a major defeat for the Soviet detente lobby. . . . I don't think our media understands this policy process in the Soviet system. And thus our commentators don't understand that American policy itself influences the outcome of these struggles within the high Soviet elite.

Finally, there is the larger media subject of the relationship between the Soviet state and Soviet society. . . .

At no time other than during a meeting of superpower leaders is the media so focused on U.S.-Soviet relations.

Kirk, *The Toledo Blade.*

THE NEWS
MEDIA

79

Do Soviets perceive a controlled press as good and a free press as bad?

What is the consensual social contract in the Soviet Union, between the ruled and rulers? To put it differently, what is the message of "communism" inside the Soviet Union? What are the domestic promises of Soviet communism? They are not Marxist in the old millennial sense. They are, instead, five more early promises that the Soviet government has made to its people in modern times. Let me be specific.

First, the government has promised the people national security — or, since 1941 it will never happen again. Second, it has promised some popular form of state nationalism. Third, it has promised law-and-order safeguards against internal disorder and anarchy. Fourth, it has promised cradle-to-grave welfarism. And fifth, it has promised that each generation will lead a better material life than the previous one. . . .

I would say, on balance, that the Soviet government, in its own clumsy way, has fulfilled most of these promises over the years. It has over-fulfilled its pledges of national security and law-and-order. It has made nationalism and patriotism major themes of what it calls communism, or Marxism-Leninism, today. It has created a crude but truly cradle-to-grave welfare system, from free health care and education to pensions. And until now, each Soviet generation has lived a better material life than its predecessor. . . .

Why, then, is American media coverage of the Soviet Union so inadequate?

Partly, . . . I think it is the old American media habit: when in doubt, always assume that the Soviet Union is wrong or guilty. Don't give them any benefit of the doubt because they lie so much. This media habit is reinforced, I think, by a persistent anxiety on the part of many journalists, and many academics, that they might appear to be too soft on the Soviet system; that they may get a reputation for being insufficiently hard-headed about Soviet reality. Partly, alas, the problem is also the media's tendency to echo the prevailing tone of American politics and

"Freedom of the Press"

J. G. Szabo, Rothco.

FREEDOM OF PRESS

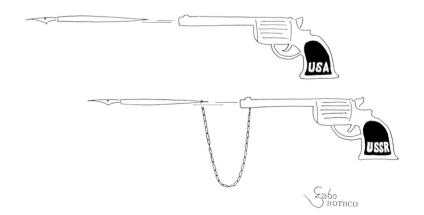

particularly, the White House. Too many of the Reagan Administration's contentions about the Soviet system, for example, are thoughtlessly parroted by the media today. For example, that the system is in crisis; or that if the Soviet Union had a real leader, we would have had an arms control agreement long ago.

And partly, I think, the problem is that the American media lacks a professional corps of Sovietologists. This differs, incidentally, from your Soviet counterparts. Soviet journalists who cover America do it more or less for life, as a profession. They're trained as Americanists, and they work either in Canada, America, or England. For better or worse we lack a professional corps of Sovietological journalists in the United States. Most journalists who cover the Soviet Union, even correspondents who go there, are amateurs. Some of them become very good, others learn very little.

But the harshest thing I want to say is that the main problem may be that the American media is lazy. Very few journalists seem to bother to read much serious literature about the Soviet Union, to inform themselves. That may be my harshest indictment: There is a vast discrepancy between the importance you attach to covering the Soviet Union, and your apparent lack of effort to become truly informed about the Soviet Union.

R eading Cohen's assessment ... was like listening through a thick wall: parts were intelligible; but too much of it, to borrow his words, was "one-dimensional, distorted, and factually wrong."

It is unfair and unconstructive not to distinguish in the first place between American reporting from Moscow and American reporting and commentary about the Soviet Union from the outside, often by people who have never set foot in the country or who, like Mr. Cohen, visit irregularly and briefly at best. Reporting from Moscow has its flaws, but he has missed or distorted most of them.

He takes as his yardstick the quality of "leaderology" reporting and cites as an example the media's brief "fixation" with Yuri Andropov's supposed Western tastes and liberalism. To the best of my knowledge, none of this came from any of the two dozen American correspondents in Moscow. . . .

Coverage of the leadership ebbed and flowed over a number of years, in keeping with the ups and downs of Brezhnev's health. It became the main priority in January of 1982 with the death of Mikhail A. Suslov, the Politburo's ideologist, whose departure — Cohen's system of checks and balances against personal power notwithstanding — clearly altered the balance of power in the leadership.

Within days it was apparent that a pre-succession power struggle had begun. By early February one could read reports from Moscow that

Robert Gillette, "American Coverage of the Soviet Union: A Reply," *Neiman Reports* (Cambridge, MA), Spring 1985.

WITH PRIDE, COMRADES, I TELL YOU THAT THE GRAND AND GLORIOUS NEW LEADERSHIP HERE IN THE KREMLIN IS PROJECTING A PICTURE OF SOVIET STABILITY.

Why, ALREADY, we've seen a decrease in mail addressed to "Occupant."

The American media, as well as professional scholars, have great difficulty interpreting the Soviet succession process.

Courtesy of Tom Gibb, *Altoona Mirror.*

Andropov was likely to leave the KGB for a more advantageous position as a central committee secretary in Suslov's place. In May, he did so.

Moscow that summer and fall was awash in conflicting hints and rumors, many of them deliberately propagated by rival elements of the leadership through the most unlikely channels. They added up to roughly equal probability that Andropov or Chernenko would be the successor. If there was confusion among journalists, it was no less among diplomats. . . .

It well may be that the cold war lobby, as Cohen puts it, has gained dominance over the detente lobby. But neither he nor we can say with any precision who stands on which side or how long the cold war viewpoint will prevail, or to what extent it represents the lowest common denominator of policy wrought by a leadership in transition. But history is littered with examples of the ability of Soviet foreign policy to turn on a dime when it serves the Soviet Union's long-term strategic interests, which Moscow probably holds in sharper focus than Washington does its own. . . .

Sitting in Moscow, it is hard to know what America's dominant view is of Soviet society. It is certainly a fallacy that economic pressures can bring the Soviet Union to its knees, but no one I know among correspondents thinks of this society as unstable. One of its remarkable features is the apparent satisfaction so many Russians feel in the face of what most of us would consider a dismal standard of living and the absence of liberties we take for granted.

It is not for nothing that Soviet statistics on the quality of life still take 1913 as their standard of reference. Russians, as Nikita Khrushchev once observed, don't ask for much.

Apart from a thin veneer of intellectuals, they also don't know very much about conditions in their own country or about alternative social systems, a testimonial to the effectiveness of information control in the Soviet Union.

Asked in a recent opinion poll to name countries other than the Soviet Union with the highest standard of living, residents of provincial Taganrog listed in rank order Czechoslovakia, the United States, East Germany, and Sweden. Candidates for "most developed democracy" outside the Soviet Union were Czechoslovakia, France, Bulgaria, and East Germany. Worst violators of human rights? Greece, the United States, Spain, and West Germany. . . .

One of many factors shaping American reporting is a compulsion to react to the torrent of misinformation and lies from the official media, both about life inside the country and outside. It is an urge to discover what the Soviet state would prefer that Westerners not know, to set the record straight. . . .

A larger part of the answer is that the problems are more visible than the achievements. Health care, for instance, is free. But medications are not, and bribery for better service is commonplace. Soviet health care, moreover, is dispensed by the world's largest corps of poorly trained doctors so miserably supplied with ordinary necessities that hospital nurses in Moscow must sometimes bring bandages from home. . . .

From the beginning of 1982 to the present [Spring 1985], two successions, the decline in U.S.-Soviet relations, the downing of the Korean airliner, and the fortunes of arms talks dictated the bulk of coverage and left comparatively little time for what should have been the most rewarding part of the job: thoughtful examination of a society in which a few of us are privileged to live for a short time.

Are correspondents as poorly prepared to cover the Soviet Union as Cohen suggests? As many as a third of them are, but it is not a question of laziness.

Some news organizations — especially wire services and television networks — seem to have a hard time recruiting qualified reporters for Moscow, and they apparently fail to see the value in unleashing those who do step forward for several months of uninterrupted preparation.

When a volunteer is found, he or she may be thrust into this unique and forbidding environment with only a few months, or even weeks, of advance notice. . . .

The disadvantaged correspondent, if he or she takes an interest in Moscow as most do, undergoes a grueling first year of on-the-job education. The normal pace of 14- to 18-hour days, six to seven days a week, becomes even more stressful than it is for better-equipped colleagues.

The result is not so much inaccurate reporting as shallow reporting. The stories lack cultural and historical context. They skirt the most interesting questions. Editors are fended off with light-weight feature stories on long lines and the surprising quality of Soviet ice cream, while reporters lean unduly on local diplomats and their colleagues for foreign policy analysis. . . .

Even the well-grounded correspondent is hard-put to keep up with the current Soviet studies, once he or she arrives in Moscow. Foreign desks pass along whatever comes floating in, but there is no systematic collecting and relaying of professional papers. . . . To a large degree, correspondents are cut off from the fund of information produced by American specialists.

Another deficiency in reporting from Moscow is the minuscule amount of air time most of the network reporters are able to scrape from editors in New York. (Cable News Network is a notable exception.) . . . Each of the networks has built up a large video library in Moscow that could do far more than print journalists can to convey the texture of Soviet life. Little of this footage, apparently, will ever be seen by the public.

Can American understanding of the Soviet Union be improved by closer relations with Soviet journalists?

To the extent . . . exchanges [of Soviet and American journalists] allow American news executives to break away from suffocating rounds of banquets and guided tours of model schools to see the Soviet Union firsthand, they can't hurt. But the premise that misunderstanding has something to do with mistrust between the superpowers needs to be examined more closely. The reverse may cut closer to the truth. . . .

Some Soviet journalists might benefit from a look at America, but the [top press] "leaders" . . . are already well versed in American affairs. So charming in person, [they] are not journalists in any meaningful sense of the word but propagandists. They are professional well-poisoners who got where they are today not by challenging the assumptions and instructions of the Central Committee but by generating calculated misunderstanding through their newspapers and on television with sufficient skill and credence to plant in a great many Soviet hearts the fear of an America bent on thermonuclear war.

Exchanging dinner toasts and small gifts with these people may leave a reassuring warmth in the hearts of some news executives on the American side, but it is unlikely to translate into fairer reporting on the Soviet side. As a Soviet journalist, in a moment of candor, explained early in my term, "Your god is information. Ours is Marxism-Leninism."

The information that comes from Moscow paints a harsh reality. The messenger could be better, but that is not likely to make the message more comforting.

The debate in America over whether the media is delivering an accurate message regarding the Soviet Union is likely to continue. The information and images of the U.S.S.R. that news organizations provide will continue to be criticized, from one perspective or another, as being either incomplete or inaccurate. With no more than two dozen bureaus from American popular news organizations in the Soviet Union — working against both self- and Soviet-imposed constraints — it may not really be surprising that we do not receive a full picture of the Soviet Union.

Whether through reports in newspapers or pictures on a TV screen, our views of the U.S.S.R. are often reinforced, and sometimes challenged, by what we watch and read. By being increasingly aware of how the Soviet and American media gather news, we can become more sensitive to the ways our perceptions are influenced by newspaper, magazines, radio, and television.

BOOKS

STORIES AND STUDIES

Messages conveyed by books — some subtle, others direct, some intended, others unconscious — contribute to Americans' and Soviets' perceptions of each other. As schoolchildren we form impressions of other people and places from what we read in lessons, stories, and textbooks. Throughout our lives we continue our education formally and informally by reading fiction, nonfiction, biographies, essays, and hundreds of things in between.

The discipline required of reading means that impressions gained through books are often long-lasting. Schoolchildren are required to study and memorize, and even reading for pleasure demands time and concentration. Books can offer a more subtle and complex view of events than can television, for example, which usually just skims visually over the surface of an issue before hurrying on to another.

Textbooks and literature, however, are not necessarily more accurate than the news media in the images they present of other countries. They too can be biased, distorting, and propagandistic. This is especially true for schoolbooks as governments play a large role in deciding curricula. Although this is a much bigger problem in the Soviet Union, where negative views of America are actively and openly encouraged, the U.S. is not free of politically motivated efforts to shape the content of textbooks and school materials.

In both countries, even before Soviet and American children study history, social studies, or civics, they develop images of the other superpower through their beginning readers. The reprint that follows is an example of an anti-American story from *Rodnaya Rech'* (Mother Tongue), a first-grade Russian-language reader currently used in Soviet schools.

What would be the possible results of an American student's using translated Soviet books and a Soviet student's using translated American books?

■ 87

"The Red Shoes," in Logan Robinson, *An American in Leningrad* (New York: W. W. Norton, 1982).

The dark-skinned little girl Nancy lived with her mother in an American city. Nancy's mother worked as a dishwasher in a restaurant and got home after midnight. But no matter how late her mother got home, Nancy always waited and did not go to bed without her.

Nancy's shoes had worn out. They were so worn out that even their neighbor, the shoemaker Bill, couldn't do anything to fix them. The sole of the left shoe was entirely torn off, and the right one had such a gaping hole that one could see the toes of Nancy's foot.

In the morning, looking over what remained of her shoes, Nancy started to cry. "How am I going to go walking without shoes?" Her mother sighed heavily, "I will stay at work until morning. Then, perhaps, I can manage to save enough money to buy you a new pair of shoes."

Until morning? Did that mean Nancy would be alone all night? But the desire to have new shoes was so strong that Nancy didn't pay any attention.

"Mama, buy me red shoes, you know, like the ones the little girl had that we saw in the park," she begged her mother. Her mother sighed once again, "I don't know, my little girl, if I'll be able to earn enough." However, Nancy so plaintively begged her mother to buy her the red shoes, without fail, that her mother at last promised.

On Nancy's mother's day off, they set out together for the shoestore. In the shining plate-glass show window of the store stood boots and shoes of all colors. Nancy was dazzled: she had never seen such elegant shoes. Suddenly she cried out, "Mama, Mama, look: there they are — the red shoes! Let's go quickly, Mama, and buy them!"

They went into the store. One salesman was trying a pair of yellow shoes on a fair-haired, snub-nosed little boy; the other salesman nonchalantly chattered away. The tall proprietor by the desk didn't even look over at the Negress with the little girl.

Nancy and her mother stood a long time by the counter. At last Nancy's mother timidly requested, "Forgive me, please, wouldn't you be so kind as to show us a pair of red shoes for my little girl?"

One of the salesmen reluctantly came over to them.

"These are expensive goods," he said. "Do you have enough money for such shoes?"

The mother showed her purse. "There, sir, all last week I worked nights." Only then the salesman laid out on the counter a pair of red shoes. They were so soft, shone so nicely, and smelled so of new leather that Nancy started clapping her hands.

The salesman growled, "You can try them on if you want."

He himself was supposed to try shoes on the customers, but he wouldn't dream of stooping for these black customers. The mother herself knelt down in front of Nancy and began to pull the shoes on her. But what a pity, they were too small.

"I wonder if you might, sir, have a little bigger pair?" requested Nancy's mother.

The salesman sullenly looked over at her. "A little larger? I have them. Only you have to take the pair you tried on."

Nancy's mother rose from her knees.

"Take this pair?" she asked again. "But really, these shoes are too tight for the little girl."

The salesman quietly wrapped up the shoes in paper. "And who would want to take these shoes, which were put on your black feet? You have to take these shoes from us."

Nancy's mother clasped her hands. "My God, really all I have is enough for one pair. Does this mean my little girl must remain without shoes?"

Hearing this, Nancy loudly started to cry. Her mother approached the proprietor of the store.

"Sir," she appealed to him. "I implore you, sir, don't make me buy these shoes . . . I don't have a spare cent, sir . . ."

"I don't want to incur a loss because of you," muttered the proprietor. "You should have known that after your little girl tried them on, not one American would buy these shoes for his children."

"You're wrong about that, proprietor," a loud, friendly voice suddenly resounded.

A customer in blue work coveralls walked up to the counter and patted Nancy on the back.

"You don't have to cry, little girl," he said. "Although the shoes you tried on were expensive, I'll take them anyway; they are perfectly suitable for my little girl. And you yourself purchase other ones. I know well the meaning of hard-earned money."

He pulled out of his pocket enough money, paid the salesman, and took up the package with the shoes. Then he bowed to Nancy's mother and walked out of the store.

Successfully and happily, Nancy and her mother returned home that day. The dark-skinned little girl rejoiced at her new red shoes, which squeaked quietly with each of her steps.

Questions to the Text:

1. What country does Nancy live in?
2. Why was it difficult for Nancy's mother to buy shoes for her daughter?
3. How did Nancy and her mother buy the shoes? Tell the story.
4. Who helped the dark-skinned customers? Read the story.
5. Explain the expression "hard-earned money."

The American who translated "The Red Shoes" described this conversation with a Soviet student, Max, who owned the book.

"Sensing my discomfort [with the story], Max assured me that all the little kids in Leningrad listened to the Voice of America Russian-language broadcasts and weren't about to believe this kind of foolishness. Everybody knew life was better in America, Max said, because even though Americans were allowed to travel, no one he knew had ever met an American who had immigrated to the Soviet Union." Max's comments about the story raise an important question: do Soviet children really believe that such stories accurately portray life in the U.S. in the 1980s?

Through history lessons, American and Soviet children gain lasting impressions of each other's country. And here, too, both sides suffer from biased or inaccurate description. As we would expect, Soviet texts explain American history through the prism of Marxist ideology. The Revolutionary War, for example, is uniformly described as a "bourgeois" revolt of wealthy American merchants and landowners against British colonialism. And the industrial revolution is described as a cruel exploitation of American workers for the profit of a few wealthy capitalists, one step down the road to an eventual Communist revolution. An excerpt from a typical Soviet eighth-grade text follows.

Reproduced from a 1985 Soviet History text, this map shows the "territorial growth of the U.S. in the first half of the nineteenth century." Vertical lines depict the "capitalist North" and intercepting lines the "slave-owning South"; slanted lines indicate "Western colonies."

Courtesy of U.S.S.R. Embassy, Washington, DC.

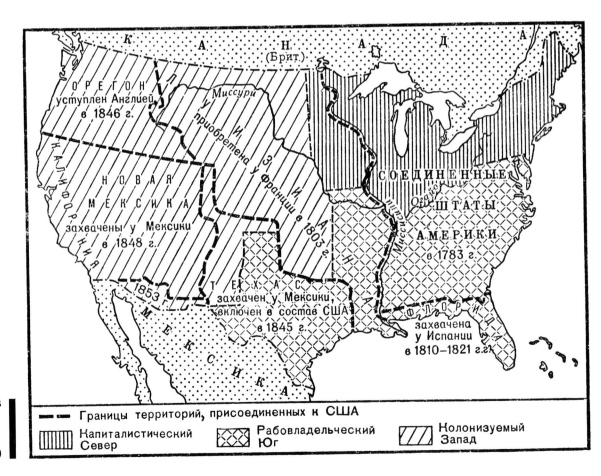

Two streams of colonizers advanced westward: from the southern states went mostly planters with their slaves, and from the northern states — farmers, among whom were many poor, dreaming of owning a scrap of land and setting up their own farm. The colonists traveled in wagon trains pulled by oxen. The road went on for months. It was especially difficult for the settlers if they lost their oxen. Here is what one settler wrote at the time: "The man threw the straps over his shoulder and dragged the cart by its shaft, the boy helped his father, the wife rode in the cart, and the old lady walked, carrying a gun and leading a cow."

The western lands, according to the Government's announcement, were not given freely to all who sought land, but were sold. The price of land was not set too high, but it was still inaccessible to the poor. Because of this many speculators got involved, buying and then selling their farmland for much higher prices. The farmers demanded the free distribution of the western lands for all who came West. Some of them, not having enough money to buy land, simply went out and settled some parts of the West.

The West attracted many immigrants from Europe. The U.S. population grew rapidly, increasing the demand for industrial trade and expanding the internal market. The opening of the West further contributed to the rapid industrialization of the North. But at the same time, the presence of open, virgin land was one cause of the expansion of slavery in the U.S.A.

The two movements of settlers collided in Kansas in 1854. Farmers from the North energetically set about working the most fertile land. From the South came the hired guns of the slaveowners. The guns thundered on the prairies. "Two men," recounted one eyewitness, "approached each other with pistols in hand. The first words asked the most important question: 'Are you for a free state or slavery?' And, as often happened, the answer to the question came with a gunshot."

"The Colonization of the West," *Novaya Istoria* (Recent History) (Moscow, 1985), Chapter 11, pp. 182–183

American educators who have studied the portrayal of the U.S. in Soviet schoolbooks cite a number of persistent problems. The following article outlines some of them.

This brief article can only skim the various problems and deficiencies the American reviewers of Soviet textbooks discovered during their investigation. The types of problems discussed below were characteristic of all of the texts and are not limited to one or two. The examples given for each problem are cited merely as illustrations and do not exhaust the number of cases uncovered by the reviewers. . . .

Howard Mehlinger, "The United States as Portrayed in Geography and History Textbooks in the USSR," *Social Education*, April 1981.

PROBLEM OF BALANCE OF TREATMENT

One question is whether the amount of treatment accorded the United States is adequate, given the purpose and scope of a textbook; a second question is whether the treatment provided is balanced or fair. In general, the reviewers found much to criticize.

Attention is focused on the least attractive aspects of American life: poverty, unemployment, inflation, crime, social inequality, racism, hedonism, and militarism. No one would deny that American society and culture contain elements of all of these, but few Americans understand these to be the dominant features of American life. But what will Soviet students conclude from their tenth-grade world history book that asserts: "It is not surprising that a typical trait of American society, which is founded on social inequality, should be violence and terror"? Or what impression will Soviet students gain of the American standard of living from their ninth-grade geography book that states: "Under the conditions of Capitalism one-third of Americans are unable to buy necessary food?"

Textbooks that provide one-sided and slanted accounts of another society leave distorted images in the minds of impressionable youth. We cannot object to Soviet textbooks including descriptions of social problems that concern many Americans, but the authors should also discuss some of the many public and private programs that have been established to resolve such problems. Nor is it fair to imply that poverty, assault, theft, alcoholism, and racism are found in capitalist societies only. What is required are textbook descriptions of both the strengths and the weaknesses of a society, together with a discussion of how and whether a country is seeking to resolve its social problems. . . .

PROBLEMS OF DISTORTION AND BIAS BY UNDUE EMPHASIS

More serious than factual errors are the bias and distortion that appear in Soviet textbooks because of undue and excessive emphasis upon a particular fact, statement, or event taken out of context and given more significance than it deserves.

An example of this problem can be found in the grade-eight world history textbook. Commenting on the attitude of white settlers toward American Indians, the author writes:

The American bourgeoisie and the slave-owners tried to seize as much foreign land as possible. First of all they began with the extermination of the Indians, in order to seize their lands. "The only good Indian is a dead Indian," said American generals. One means of exterminating the Indians was the following: Blankets were strewn about near an Indian settlement. The Indians, not suspecting anything, gathered them up and covered themselves with them. Then they began to die in masses from smallpox — it turned out that the Americans had wrapped up those who were sick with or had died from smallpox beforehand in the blankets.

> Is there a "right" and a "wrong" portrayal of history, or is all history subjective?

Thus, by the 19th century the American military was already using methods of monstrous bacteriological warfare.

No one would deny that the Indians were often exploited and mistreated, and it *may* be true that smallpox-infected blankets were once used to decimate Indians, although American historians are not agreed that this was ever done. But, even if it did occur, it does not justify the far-fetched conclusion that this was a result of a conscious policy to conduct bacteriological warfare on the part of the American military, a policy the author asserts continues to the present time. No purpose can be served by such a statement other than to poison the attitudes of Soviet youth toward the United States.

Soviet educators, similarly, have a number of complaints regarding the portrayal of their country in American schoolbooks. Probably the most frequent Soviet complaint is that Russian and Soviet history is largely ignored in American schools. The Soviet junior high school textbook mentioned earlier, *Novaya Istoria,* devotes over thirty pages to American history in its discussion of events in the late eighteenth and nineteenth centuries. Few American textbooks devote more than a few paragraphs to Russia or the U.S.S.R. This is one of the major reasons that despite Americans' access to a multitude of independently published textbooks, Soviet citizens are taught far more about the U.S. than we are about the Soviet Union.

Another complaint lodged against American schoolbooks is that the Soviet role in world history is often ignored or denigrated to the point of complete inaccuracy. This problem is probably most acute in our schoolbooks' description of World War II. Although the Soviets engaged most of Hitler's armies between 1941 and 1944, and had turned the tide against the Nazis by 1943, the American view of World War II focuses on what the Soviets consider the secondary theaters of war, North Africa and the Pacific. Of the more than 28 pages devoted to the World War II in an American high school textbook, *The European World* (Boston: Little, Brown, 1970), fewer than four pages discuss the Soviet role in defeating Hitler. Stalin is almost entirely ignored when the Allied leaders are mentioned. Because the war was such a devastating experience for the Soviet Union and the Soviet contribution to Hitler's defeat was so enormous (some 20,000,000 Soviets perished during the war), Soviet educators are offended by textbooks that, to them, belittle the Soviet role in Hitler's defeat.

Another example of a significant omission in the teaching of Soviet history is found in the excerpt below. Its description of the Bolshevik revolution and civil war entirely ignores the allied intervention — despite the fact that allies sent more than 100,000 soldiers into Russia, including some 10,000 Americans.

Should history textbooks try to avoid reflecting prevailing national political perspectives?

Carl Becker and Kenneth Cooper, *Modern History* (Morristown, NJ: Silver Burdett, 1977), pp. 427–428, 449–450.

On November 7, 1917, the Bolsheviks overthrew the provisional government of Russia in a second revolution. The Bolsheviks won support from a war-weary people by promising peace, so the next month they declared a truce with the Central Powers.

The Russian Revolution, which at first encouraged the Allies, proved to be a disaster to them. Never were the Allies more discouraged than in the summer and fall of 1917. The United States had declared war [on Germany], but was as yet of little aid. Russia, instead of renewing the war with vigor, was spreading the doctrine of "peace with no annexations and no indemnities." Worst of all, the doctrine found adherents in France and England . . . .

When the Bolsheviks, or Communists, overthrew the provisional government in Russia in November, 1917, they were only a small group. They by no means had the support of any large number of Russians. The Communists had to fight for power against a number of groups, including several armies led by former tsarist generals. For nearly three years Russia was torn by a cruel civil war, which added to the misery of the long-suffering Russian people. It was not until 1920 that the Communists finally managed to get control of the country.

The ultimate Communist victory was remarkable, because at no time before or during the civil war did the Communists make up more than a tiny minority of the Russian people. That this small group managed to acquire control of a nation of 130 million people was due in part to the shrewd abilities of a man whose real name was Vladimir Ilyich Ulyanov, but who is best known by his alias, Nikolai Lenin.

Do Soviet and American textbooks ignore positive aspects of each nation for similar or different reasons?

In 1981 a joint U.S.-Soviet project examined each nation's textbooks. The following is an excerpt from recommendations made by the U.S.S.R. Ministry of Education.

"U.S./U.S.S.R. Textbook Study Project," *Interim Report*, June 1981.

Socialism was built in the U.S.S.R. during an exceptionally difficult international situation. It seems essential for the [American] textbooks to supply a more comprehensive analysis of the causes of World War II and to show how the Soviet Union consistently advocated a system of collective security in Europe in the face of the growing threat of war posed by Nazism. There is a need for a well-balanced presentation of all of the foreign policy actions of the Soviet Union, on the one hand, and Britain and France, on the other, on the eve of World War II. Textbooks should stress in particular that the U.S.S.R. concluded a non-aggression treaty with Germany in 1939 only after all of its attempts to reach agreement on an alliance with the Western powers had failed and after it had become clear that the Western states had no serious intention to conclude such an alliance.

It is necessary to supply all facts clearly indicating that all of the

subsequent steps taken by the U.S.S.R., up to the moment when Nazi Germany attacked it (among them the armed conflict with Finland), were in no way aggressive actions but were required by the need to strengthen the country's defenses.

World War II, unleashed by the Nazis, was a severe trial for all mankind. The burden of the war was carried by the Soviet people, who lost 20 million lives in it. Soviet experts believe it is fundamentally important to demonstrate the decisive role played by the U.S.S.R. in defeating the main force of aggression, Nazi Germany.

Between 1941 and 1944, the main theatre of operations was at the Soviet-German front, where major battles at Moscow, Stalingrad, and the Kursk Bulge were of primary importance to the outcome of the war. That is why it seems worthwhile to cite comparative statistics on the forces of the antagonists in various parts of the world and at various stages of the war, and also on the losses inflicted on the aggressor by the allies, in order to present objectively the character and course of combat operations.

It is likewise desirable to characterize in greater detail military coop-

Access to the collection in the Lenin Library in Moscow is limited to people with particular research tasks, and specific materials are provided on a "need- to-know" basis.
Sovfoto.

eration between the U.S.S.R., the U.S.A. and Britain, and also the nature of American aid to the U.S.S.R. Accurate data should be supplied on Lend-Lease deliveries and on their share of the total volume of armaments available to the Soviet Union at various stages of the war. It is important to stress the Soviet Union's faithfulness to its commitments as an ally, including its prompt and timely entrance into the war with Japan.

Particular emphasis should be laid on the fact that during World War II the U.S.S.R. and the U.S.A. were able to put aside their political and ideological differences and to work successfully as allies in the struggle against all the forces of aggression.

In addition to portrayals of history, interesting insights into how Americans and Soviets see each other's countries can be gleaned from their reactions to literature. An American description of J. D. Salinger's classic and controversial novel, *The Catcher in the Rye*, is followed by impressions of the same book written by two Soviet high school students.

Charlotte A. Alexander, *Monarch Notes on* The Catcher in the Rye (New York: Monarch Press, 1965), pp. 16, 41–42.

We find that one of the most oft-used words in Holden's lexicon is "phony." He is constantly detecting sham motives in the people around him. The advertisement for Pencey Prep disturbs him; the picture of a horse jumping over a fence gives, in his opinion, a false image of the school. In Holden's judgment, Pencey is a home for dishonest, spoiled children, and not for idealized horsemen-to-be. . . . One of the most important and revealing sections of the novel involves Holden's arrival at his home. At last Holden is beginning to formulate his thoughts — a bit incoherently, it is true — about what he wants to do with his life. The "Catcher in the Rye" is the guardian of innocence and the protector of innocents. Thus, we discern Salinger's oft-implied creed — the human animal is pure childhood; he is not corrupted until he enters adult society. Whatever unpleasant characteristics a child may display are the results of premature exposure to adult influence — which may remind us of Holden's prematurely gray hair. This idea is a slight variation of Rousseau's concept of the "Noble Savage."

Dmitry Shenshin, student essay on *Catcher in the Rye* excerpted from translations in the *U.S.-U.S.S.R. Youth Exchange Program Lesson Book*, (U.S.A.: Tides Foundation/U.S.-U.S.S.R. Youth Exchange Program, 1984), p. III–6.

After I have read this book I understand how hard it is to live in the world where everything is sold and bought. The main hero of this novel, Holden Caulfield, came across with all troubles American society of that time: loneliness, failure to understand — is quite the problems of that teenagers.

He understands how phony is the world which surrounds him. He understood and he tried to fight against this show-offy rubbish. But the trouble is that he can't oppose anything to that society structure. He can put forward his really wonderful credo: "I keep picturing all these little kids playing some games in this high field of rye and all. Thousands of little kids, and nobody's around — nobody big, I mean — except me. And I'm standing on the edge of some crazy cliff. What I have to do, I have to catch everybody if they start to go over the cliff. I mean if they're running and they don't look where they're going. I have to come out from somewhere and catch them. That's all I'd do all day, I'd just be the catcher in the rye. I know it's crazy, but that's the only thing I'd really like to be. I know it is crazy."

In plainer words, Holden wants to hold back kids from adulthood, he wants to save them from this world. But he knew that he can't apply this wonderful credo in life. But he really loves kids, so these qualities of his character can make him in future an excellent teacher or a brilliant psychoanalyst. His other problem was that people don't understand him even when he spoke with them about the ducks in Central Park, or when he was speaking with "five dollars girl."

The only man whom Holden revealed his heart and soul was Mr. Antolini. He gave Holden a key to the solution of that problem. Only Mr. Antolini knew well how to deal with Caulfield's soul. And, after all, Mr. Antolini makes believe Holden that he *can* become a personality, a person useful for humanity.

For Soviets of all ages, reading is a favorite pastime.

SIPA/Special Features.

V. Emelianov, student essay on *Catcher in the Rye* excerpted from translations in the *U.S.-U.S.S.R. Youth Exchange Program Lesson Book*, (U.S.A.: Tides Foundation/U.S.-U.S.S.R. Youth Exchange Program, 1984), p. III–10.

We can find, that "The Catcher in the Rye" is very rich and illustrative of the obscure human problems. And one of the most important problems, touched in this book, is the main idea, which was expressed by the author in the title.

The hero of this book, Holden Caulfield, realizes that he can't apply himself in life. But, it isn't true. We can see, that Holden is a very smart guy, but he doesn't learn hard because of permanent and endless conflicts with all that "phony" world around him.

Many qualities of Holden may help him find his future way in his life. In his talk with his sister Phoebe, when she asked him what he would like to do in future, he answered, that he'd like to be a "catcher in the rye."

To be a "catcher in the rye," to save people, especially the children — that is all Holden wants. He wants, in plainer words, to work in the name of human beings, to help people, when they are in danger, or in the need.

We can see, that Holden loves children. This quality can make him in future, a good teacher or psychologist.

Mr. Antolini was the only "ideal teacher" in Holden's life (according to Holden) but Holden doesn't make a mistake, when he thinks so. Mr. Antolini is not only a teacher, but he is a brilliant psychologist. He gives Holden a key to the solution of his problem. He says, that Holden has no right to stop learning: "I have a feeling, that you are riding for some kind of a terrible fall. . . ."

Mr. Antolini knows well, how to deal with Holden. He says that only educated and scholarly men are able to contribute something valuable to the world. And, after all, he makes Holden believe in his own abilities.

Because, if one doesn't believe in his own mental power, then what he can do for the human beings and for himself. For now we know, that Holden can become a person useful for humanity. He really can.

American literature, including novels like *The Catcher in the Rye,* is a large part of the Soviet school curriculum. Soviet students and adults read (in English or in translation) the classic works of such American authors as James Fenimore Cooper, Edgar Allen Poe, Washington Irving, Walt Whitman, Henry Wadsworth Longfellow, Mark Twain, Jack London, Eugene O'Neill, John Steinbeck, and Ernest Hemingway. By contrast, many American students know only the work of Tolstoy or Dostoevsky from the wealth of Russian literature and poetry. This disparity holds for contemporary writers. The works of Kurt Vonnegut, James Baldwin, John Updike, Joyce Carol Oates, William Styron, John Cheever, and Studs Terkel are available in the Soviet Union. Soviet publishers have now produced 35 volumes of a projected 45-volume Library of Translated American Literature. Reading these authors, many Soviet citizens have a richer perspective on our nation than Americans do of Russia. It is true that the Soviet authorities tend to publish in Russian only those writers whose works portray the more difficult aspects of American life, but even within these constraints, readers are able to grasp the complexity and variety of life in the U.S.

Many other American books might be published in the Soviet Union were it not for certain obstacles raised by the Soviet authorities. For example, the Soviets were interested in publishing Jonathan Schell's recent *The Fate of the Earth* but insisted on removing certain passages and references to emigré author Alexander Solzhenitsyn. Schell and his American publisher refused, so the project came to a halt. An even more curious case involved E. L. Doctorow's *Ragtime.* The book was well on its way toward publication in Russian when its translator, writer Vasily Aksyonov, fell from favor with the Soviet literary establishment. For reasons that have nothing to do with the book, therefore, *Ragtime* remains unpublished in the Soviet Union.

In addition to those American books officially approved and published by the Soviet government, there also exists a thriving black market in unapproved or "banned" American authors. According to one Russian emigré now living in New York, as many American books are smuggled into the Soviet Union illegally as are published officially. If true, this means that of the American books owned by Soviet citizens, half are read in English!

Because many more Soviets know English than Americans know Russian, they are able to learn more easily about us. According to another emigré, one of the most popular books on the Soviet black market is *The Russians,* written by Hedrick Smith, a former Moscow correspondent. The book's frank assessment of Soviet life is intolerable for

The circular central reading room of the Library of Congress in Washington continues today, as it has in the past, to attract scholars and students from around the world.

Courtesy of the Library of Congress.

Soviet authorities. Soviet readers, however, are interested in how Americans view the U.S.S.R. — so interested that they are willing to pay as much as 75 rubles (out of an average monthly salary of 190 rubles) for a single used paperback copy. Although it is much in demand in the Soviet Union, *The Russians* has also been one of the most popular recent sources of information about the Soviet Union for many Americans. The book offers a rich and detailed look at the complexity of life in the U.S.S.R. Published in 1976, *The Russians* spent over six months on the *New York Times* bestseller list.

Unfortunately, contemporary Soviet literature has yet to attract many American readers, despite bold works by such authors as Valentin Rasputin and Chingiz Aitmatov, which are available in English. Even the critically acclaimed books of Soviet emigrés such as Vladimir Voinovich (*The Ivankiad, The Life and Extraordinary Adventures of Private Ivan Chonkin*), Sergei Dovlatov (*The Compromise*), and Vasily Aksyonov (*The Burn, The Island of Crimea*) sell relatively few copies in the U.S. The immense popularity of American books in the Soviet Union is partly due to the fact that American literature offers a rich and stimulating view of life in America which is largely unavailable in the U.S.S.R. The overwhelming popularity of the American exhibits at the annual Moscow International Book Fair is an example of this interest. According to one of the organizers of the 1985 American exhibition, Sophie Silberberg, "The Russians know a hell of a lot more about us than we know about them. We saw and touched over 35,000 Russians in one week, and gave away over 600 catalogs per hour. They are hungry about us, they care a great deal. They are interested in our authors, our concerns, our lifestyles."

The catalog Silberberg mentions is remarkable in that it is itself a book about America. *America Through American Eyes* contains brief descriptions in both English and Russian of hundreds of current American books. The free distribution of over 35,000 of these catalogs, excerpts of which follow, was like the publication of a book on American life.

Trade unions, also known as labor unions, are the principal institution — the voice, bargaining agent, protector of rights, provider of benefits — of workers in capitalist societies. After bloody battles between laborers and management's hired hands in the late nineteenth and early twentieth centuries, unions became a strong force in America's industrial society. Today, unions are facing a loss of membership and public esteem as many people, both conservative and liberal, come to view them as monopolies whose main function is to raise members' wages at the expense of the general public. In this ground-breaking study, two Harvard economics professors challenge this opinion and, with voluminous data, demonstrate that unions play a crucial and largely beneficial role in improving workplaces, increasing productivity, stabilizing the work force, and reducing inequality in our economic system. What's more, these improvements tend to spread out to benefit nonunion workers and society as a whole.

Richard B. Freeman and James L. Medoff, *What Do Unions Do?* (New York: Basic Books), reviewed in *America Through American Eyes,* (New York: Association of American Publishers, 1985).

The latest edition of what rural Americans in simpler times called "The Wish Book," the Sears Roebuck catalog is an enormous illustrated compendium of tools, clothing, dishwashers, toasters, playthings, etc., which can be bought through the mails. The book is in fact a store at which anyone can browse endlessly without spending a penny or bothering any salesperson. This business began with one man who got the idea of selling cheap but reliable watches through the mail.

Sears Roebuck and Co., *Mail Order Catalog, Illustrated* (Sears Roebuck, 1984), reviewed in *America Through American Eyes* (New York: Association of American Publishers, 1985).

Of course, many Soviet and American citizens also read popular fiction. Novels of adventure, romances,and spy thrillers are as popular in the U.S.S.R. as in the U.S. What kinds of images of each other do we get from such fiction? Not surprisingly, most portrayals of Americans in Soviet popular fiction, and vice versa, tend to reinforce stereotypes. The following translated excerpt from a Soviet novel about the adventures of Soviet teenagers traveling to the Arctic contains an interesting mix of stereotypes with a message that is surprisingly positive.

I have to admit, the plan to check out the red-haired mute kid was cooked up by Fedya and me. Holding a bright-colored scarf belonging to the "mute one," Fedya examined the firm's label, which was from Chicago, Illinois. We knew very well what "made in the USA" meant.

When I found out about this, I got mad. Where did this red-haired kid get such stuff? Maybe he's from there himself! His pants and shirt look like it, but isn't it strange that this little American can travel without a ticket on the Trans-Siberian Railway in this day and age?

Of course it's strange. Still, it doesn't hurt to remember that there were times during the Great Patriotic War [World War II] when Amer-

Aleksandr Kazantsev, *Underwater Sun* (Moscow: Soviet Russia, 1970), Chapter 7: "Made in USA."

ican boys ran to our country, very much like in pre-Revolutionary times, when Russian schoolkids tried to run away to America. I don't know how many Russian kids made it, but American kids twice got as far as Moscow.

But how did those American kids make it without knowing the language in a strange country since they were, for all practical purposes, mute? The strange riddle struck me. . . .

The kids pressed the supposed mute one to the edge of the river. He

SELECTED RUSSIAN TRANSLATIONS OF MAJOR U.S. PROSE AUTHORS (1970–1975)

Maurice Friedberg, *American Literature Through the Filter of Recent Soviet Publishing and Criticism* (Washington, DC: U.S. Information Agency, 1976).

Asimov, Isaac. *The Whiff of Death.*

Baldwin, James. *Short Stories and Essays.*

Bradbury, Ray. *Science Fiction.*

Buchwald, Art. *This Is America.*

Caldwell, Erskine. *Love and Money.*

Capote, Truman. *The Grass Harp and Short Stories.*

Cooper, James Fenimore. *The Deerslayer.*

Dreiser, Theodore. *Collected Works* in 12 volumes.

Faulkner, William. *The Golden Land.*

———. *The Sound and the Fury.*

Fitzgerald, F. Scott. *Tender Is the Night.*

Gregory, Dick. *Nigger.*

Halberstram, David. *One Very Hot Day.*

Hemingway, Ernest. *Islands in the Stream.*

———. *The Old Man and the Sea.*

———. *A Farewell to Arms.*

Hersey, John. Chapters from *Hiroshima.*

Irving, Washington. *Novellas.*

James, Henry. Novellas and short stories.

Lewis, Sinclair. *Babbit* and *Arrowsmith.*

London, Jack. Novellas and short stories.

McCullers, Carson. *The Heart Is a Lonely Hunter.*

Mailer, Norman. "The Dead Filippino."

Melville, Herman. *White Jacket.*

Oates, Joyce Carol. Stories from the collection *The Wheel of Love.*

O'Connor, Flannery. *A Good Man Is Hard to Find.*

———. *A Belated Meeting with an Adversary.*

Poe, Edgar Allan. *Complete Collection of Short Stories.*

Roth, Philip. *When She Was Good.*

Swados, Harvey. *Tales.*

Twain, Mark. *Huckleberry Finn.*

———. *Tom Sawyer.*

Vonnegut, Kurt. *Slaughterhouse-Five or the Children's Crusade.*

———. *Cat's Cradle.*

Wilder, Thorton. *The Bridge of San Luis Rey.*

Wolfe, Thomas. *The Web and the Rock.*

couldn't run away. For a while he kept looking from side to side, seeing if there was a way out, and then he started speaking his own language rapidly.

Fedya understood him.

"He says we're not bad kids. He admits that he is taking a trip around the world and is going from Baltimore to Moscow."

"Is he riding in the sleeping car?" Vitya was jealously interested. Nobody paid him any attention.

"His name is Michael. He says that he has an aunt in Baltimore," Fedya continued translating, "and that she looks like an old lamp, except that she's got a loudspeaker instead of a lightbulb. She drives you crazy, but you can't turn her off. He lived with her and her son Jerry. Jerry is mean and spiteful, but he had to live with them because his father died in the Dirty War [Vietnam]. He doesn't remember his mother at all."

"How did he make it to Russia?" Fedya translated the question and the answer.

"He took a ship out of San Francisco, and after that it's his secret. He's not the first to do this, and he really wanted to see Russia."

"So he didn't come looking for gold," surmised Galya, "but just to look at our country, which was the first to send up a sputnik."

"Oh, sputnik," Michael brightened up.

Fedya translated Michael's story about how the ship on which he'd stowed away was on its way to Vladivostok. . . . He went down the anchor chain and swam to shore. He was lucky that the border guards didn't notice him. The kids had forgotten about their bonfire, and it started to sputter out. The dampness started to waft in off the water.

"Big deal. So he swam across the bay," said Vitya. "Why doesn't he swim across this river?" Fedya translated, and Michael answered that if Moscow or Leningrad were on the other side, and there were no other way of getting there, then he would swim across.

"Good guy!" said Alyosha, clapping Michael on the back.

"It's too bad he doesn't have a passport," sighed Dennis. "What should we do with him. Hide him?"

"No, that won't do," Alyosha decided. . . .

"So how are we going to decide?" I asked.

"He'll sneak off tonight and there won't be anything to decide," said Vitya. Even I was thinking that he might run off since his secret is out.

"We have to help him," decided Alyosha. "We'll offer him a choice. Stay a vagabond or write to the proper authorities."

"He should write to the U.S. Consulate," I said.

We decided to find out what Michael wanted. . . .

The question about when some gentlemen from the consulate would come for the little American citizen, it seemed, didn't interest Michael at all. He delightedly played Indians with the kids and even swam in the river that was already cold for this time of year. The kids did not make any special effort to teach him Russian, but as he socialized with them

"Illiteracy Is Blindness"

Courtesy of U.S.S.R. Embassy, Washington, DC.

"They are hungry about us, they care a great deal. They are interested in our authors, our concerns, our lifestyles."
American organizer, International Book Fair (1985)

more and more, Michael quickly found himself in conversation with them without the help of Fedya.

What will become of this clever and brave young lad — having pretended he was mute, and even plotted the steps of his around-the-world journey?

A somewhat more stereotyped view of the Soviets is revealed in the following passage from a recent popular American novel about the crew of a Soviet nuclear submarine that defects, boat and all.

Tom Clancy, *The Hunt for Red October* (New York: Berkley Books, 1984), pp. 3–6.

S o, my Captain, again we go to sea to serve and protect the *Rodina* [Motherland]!" Captain Second Rank Ivan Yurievich Putin poked his head through the hatch — without permission, as usual — and clambered up the ladder with the awkwardness of a landsman. The tiny control station was already crowded enough with the captain, the navigator, and a mute lookout. Putin was the ship's *zampolit* (political officer). Everything he did was to serve the *Rodina* . . . a word that had mystical connotations to a Russian and, along with V. I. Lenin, was the Communist party's substitute for a godhead.

"Indeed, Ivan," Ramius replied with more good cheer than he felt. "Two weeks at sea. It is good to leave the dock. A seaman belongs at sea, not tied alongside, overrun with bureaucrats and workmen with dirty boots. And we will be warm."

"You find this cold?" Putin asked incredulously.

For the hundredth time Ramius told himself that Putin was the perfect political officer. His voice was always too loud, his humor too affected. He never allowed a person to forget what he was. The perfect political officer, Putin was an easy man to fear.

"I have been in submarines too long, my friend. I grow accustomed to moderate temperatures and a stable deck under my feet." Putin did not notice the veiled insult. He'd been assigned to submarines after his first tour on destroyers had been cut short by chronic seasickness — and perhaps because he did not resent the close confinement aboard submarines, something that many men cannot tolerate.

"Ah, Marko Aleksandrovich, Gorky on a day like this, flowers bloom!"

"And what sort of flowers might those be, Comrade Political Officer?" Ramius surveyed the fjord through his binoculars. At noon the sun was barely over the southeast horizon, casting orange light and purple shadows along the rocky walls.

"Why, snow flowers, of course," Putin said, laughing loudly. "On a day like this the faces of the children and the women glow pink, your breath trails behind you like a cloud, and the vodka tastes especially fine. Ah, to be in Gorky on a day like this!"

The bastard ought to work for Intourist, Ramius told himself, except

What would it be like, as is common in the Soviet Union, to seek out and read an officially banned book?

RUSSIAN LITERATURE IN AMERICA

Most frequently, an American course in Modern Russian Literature in English Translation begins with the year 1881. The following are the authors and works *most likely* to appear on the required reading list for each of the two semesters. The actual reading list reflects . . . the tastes of the instructor teaching the course, and may therefore vary even within a single institution. The first semester usually deals with the period from 1881 to the 1920's and the reading list may look as follows:

Chekhov, four major plays, several late novellas.
Bunin, "The Gentleman from San Francisco," *The Village.*
Kuprin, *The Duel.*
Gorky, *Childhood* and *Mother.*
Andreyev, "The Seven Who Were Hanged," "The Governor."
Blok, "The Twelve," "The Scythians."
Bely, *Petersburg.*
Sologub, *The Petty Demon.*
Remizov, selected short works.
Babel, *Red Cavalry* and *Tales of Odessa.*
Fadeyev, *The Rout.*

Mayakovsky, *The Bedbug* and selected poetry.
Zamyatin, *We.*
Zoshchenko, selected short stories.

The reading list for the second semester is likely to approximate the following:

Ehrenburg, *Julio Jurenito.*
Nabokov, *The Gift.*
Olesha, *Envy.*
Gladkov, *Cement.*
Katayev, *Time, Forward!*
Ostrovsky, N., *How the Steel was Tempered.*
Ilf and Petrov, *The Twelve Chairs.*
Sholokhov, *Silent Don* (first part).
Bulgakov, *Master and Margarita.*
Simonov, *Days and Nights.*
Stalinism, A Tragic View: Solzhenitsyn, One Day in the Life of Ivan Denisovich.
Stalinism, A Comic View: Voinovich, Private Chonkin.
The New Short Prose: Kazakov, Nagibin, Aksenov.
The New Poets: Voznesensky, Akhmadulina, Yevtushenko.
The New Drama: Arbuzov, An Irkutsk Story.

Maurice Friedberg, "The Availability of Soviet Russian Literature in the United States," for U.S. Helsinki Watch Committee, 1980.

that Gorky is a city closed to foreigners. He had been there twice. It had struck him as a typical Soviet city, full of ramshackle buildings, dirty streets, and ill-clad citizens. As it was in most Russian cities, winter was Gorky's best season. The snow hid all the dirt.

"Where we are going, Ivan Yurievich, it will be colder still."

Putin clapped his captain's shoulder. Was his affection feigned or real? Marko wondered. Probably real. Ramius was an honest man, and he recognized that this short, loud oaf did have some human feelings.

"Why is it, Comrade Captain, that you always seem glad to leave the *Rodina* and go to sea?"

Ramius smiled behind his binoculars. "A seaman has one country, Ivan Yurievich, but two wives. You never understand that. Now I go to my other wife, the cold, heartless one that owns my soul." Ramius paused. The smile vanished. "My only wife, now."

Putin was quiet for once, Marko noted. The political officer had been there, had cried real tears as the coffin of polished pine rolled into the cremation chamber. For Putin the death of Natalia Bogdanova Ramius had been a cause of grief, but beyond that the act of an uncaring God whose existence he regularly denied. For Ramius it had been a crime committed not by God but the State. An unnecessary, monstrous crime, one that demanded punishment.

"Ice." The lookout pointed.

AMERICAN BOOKS IN RUSSIA

New York Times Moscow correspondent Serge Schmemann, who informally surveyed Soviet citizens about their images of American, found that books have played an important role in Soviet perceptions of the United States.

Serge Schmemann, "The View from Russia," *The New York Times Magazine*, November 10, 1985, pp. 52-58.

The first images of America to gain wide dissemination in the Soviet Union — ones that survive to this day — were created by Soviet poets and writers who traveled to the United States. [Their writings] supplied the pioneering pictures of rapacious monopolists and soaring skyscrapers, industrious workers and throbbing factories, millionaires and beggars. They became a source of indelible images against which all subsequent perceptions have been tested. . . .

Rare is the Russian who was not reared on "The Deerslayer" and "The Adventures of Tom Sawyer," who is not familiar with "The Catcher in the Rye," Ernest Hemingway, William Faulkner and John Steinbeck. Classics and contemporary American literature are a mainstay of the Soviet reading diet, either through dog-eared copies or through translations in the enormously popular monthly journal *Foreign Literature*. . . .

[According to one Russian], "It would not be an exaggeration to say that in childhood we all were reared on American adventure literature — James Fenimore Cooper, Jack London, Edgar Allen Poe, Mark Twain, O. Henry — a whole constellation of names . . . All subsequent attitudes toward Americans are bent through this prism — not consciously, of course. Every person looks at the world in his own way, but we all played at cowboys and Indians in our childhood."

"Loose-pack ice, starboard side of the channel, or perhaps something calved off the east-side glacier. We'll pass well clear," Kamarov said.

"Captain!" The bridge speaker had a metallic voice. "Message from fleet headquarters."

"Read it."

" 'Exercise area clear. No enemy vessels in vicinity. Proceed as per orders. Signed, Korov, Fleet Commander.' "

"Acknowledged," Ramius said. The speaker clicked off. "So, no *Amerikantsi* about?"

"You doubt the fleet commander?" Putin inquired.

"I hope he is correct," Ramius replied, more sincerely than his political officer would appreciate. "But you remember our briefings."

Putin shifted on his feet. Perhaps he was feeling the cold.

"Those American 688-class submarines, Ivan, the *Los Angeles*es. Remember what one of their officers told our spy? That they could sneak up on a whale and bugger it before it knew they were there? I wonder how the KGB got that bit of information. A beautiful Soviet agent, trained in the ways of the decadent West, too skinny, the way the imperialists like their women, blond hair . . ." The captain grunted amusement. "Probably the American officer was a boastful boy, trying to find a way to do something similar to our agent, no? And feeling his liquor, like most sailors. Still. The American *Los Angeles* class, and the new British *Trafalgar*s, those we must guard against. They are a threat to us."

"The Americans are good technicians, Comrade Captain," Putin said, "but they are not giants. Their technology is not so awesome. *Nasha lutcha* [ours is better]," he concluded.

Ramius nodded thoughtfully, thinking to himself that *zampoliti* really ought to know something about the ships they supervised, as mandated by Party doctrine.

"Ivan, didn't the farmers around Gorky tell you it is the wolf you do not see that you must fear? But don't be overly concerned. With this ship we will teach them a lesson, I think."

> **"Translators are the posthorses of enlightenment."**
> **Alexander Pushkin**

Whether popular spy novels or school texts, Soviet and American books affect — in complex and sometimes unclear ways — our perceptions of each other. The ways in which they influence us may be different from the ways in which television and film (the subject of the next chapter) affect us, but even in this age of telecommunications, reading remains a primary method of learning and understanding.

More often than not, textbooks reflect the prevailing views of the society that publishes them; they reinforce common perceptions. Literature tends to be more varied, probing and exploring characters and social situations. The more aware we are of the messages in our own and other nations' books, the easier it becomes to understand why we and the Soviets think in the ways we do.

FILMS

LARGER-THAN-LIFE IMAGES

The cinema, with its sweeping scale and larger-than-life images, has also contributed to the perceptions that Americans and Soviets have of each other. For seventy-odd years, citizens of both countries have been watching and learning about each other through the eyes of filmmakers. By importing each other's films we occasionally gain insight into each other's national life and world view. More often, however, American and Soviet citizens get their cinematic impressions of each other through domestically produced movies.

Hollywood's portrayal of the Soviets, and the Soviet cinema's representation of Americans, have ranged from being surprisingly accurate to absurdly distorted. These portrayals have generally followed the swings in U.S.-Soviet relations. The most sympathetic movie images have emerged during times of cooperation, such as World War II; the most derogatory stereotypes have been produced in times of cold war and confrontation.

The following article, published in 1983, chronicles the treatment of Soviet subjects by the American movie industry and anticipates the rash of anti-Soviet movies produced in the mid-1980s.

> **"Citizens of both countries learn about each other through the eyes of filmmakers"**

I t really says something when the only progress being made in U.S.-Soviet relations is on the film front. A baby step toward detente, you might think, but a step all the same and one worth heeding when you consider the alternative offered in the Doomsday movies so prevalent now [1983].

Historically, the American screen has been sensitive to hot- and cold-running wars, mirroring the mood of the times from our own particular national perspective. This selective, filtered view has often left the made-in-Hollywood Russian without a humanistic leg to stand on, so

Harry Hann, "Seeing Red: How Hollywood Movies Handle the Russians," *New York Daily News*, December 11, 1983.

that he seems nothing more than a cardboard plot-pawn.

If screen Soviets are acquiring some shading of late, that may be because film makers no longer feel compelled to comply with the governmental view of current events — though it will be interesting to see if the current American-Russian antagonism inspires a new wave of anti-Soviet sentiment in future films.

Michael Apted's "Gorky Park" . . . is a humanistic case in point, chock full of Red herrings. There are good Russians and there are bad Russians here, just as there are — like it or lump it — good Americans and bad Americans. The hero (played by William Hurt) is a decent, dedicated Soviet police detective solving the mystery of three mutilated bodies found buried under the snow in Moscow's Gorky Park, pressing on stubbornly to the solution even when it appears the murders may be the dirty work of the KGB. Neither ideologue nor Communist, he is merely a Russian who loves his country and remains loyal to it to The End.

Such is not the screen's standard-brand Soviet. Hollywood has conditioned us to expect *dis*loyalty and defection from its Russians. It's a time-honored contrivance, never out of date. . . .

Over the years, movie Russians have run hot and cold as well. The passionate variety appeared in the pre-Revolutionary costumes, carried away in dizzy swirls of spectacle. These movies sprang either from historical events ("Rasputin and the Empress," "Nicholas and Alexandra," various Catherine the Great dramas) or from literary masterworks ("The Brothers Karamazov," "War and Peace," "Anna Karenina").

A few post-Revolutionary sagas continued in that grandly romantic manner ("Anastasia," "Reds," "Doctor Zhivago"), but, mostly, the Russian stereotype who emerged after the fall of the Romanoffs leveled off into a bloodless, bureaucratic breed, practically doubled up with the bends after that steep fall from glory. This new movie Russian had his shoulder to the wheel and both feet on the ground.

The best of both worlds and easily the most beloved of movie Russians is Nina Ivanovna Yakushova — "Ninotchka" (1939) — who received Greta Garbo's most enchanting portrayal. The role of a grimly efficient Russian envoy dovetailed perfectly with the actress' Sphinx-like image, and director Ernst Lubitsch had lyrical fun placing the humorless star in humorous situations; when she slowly warms to Western ways under the spell of Paris and Melvyn Douglas, the metamorphosis is mesmerizing. Cyd Charisse went the same amorous route (less magically, naturally) with Fred Astaire in the musical remake, Cole Porter's "Silk Stockings."

Between these two films, there were numerous "Ninotchka" ripoffs. In the 1940's "Comrade X," an uncomfortably unclarified comedy/drama, foreign correspondent Clark Gable married Russian motorman [sic] Hedy Lamarr and smuggled her out of Russia; 13 years later, in a tenser time, he pulled the same trick with his *ballerina* bride (Gene Tierney) in a thriller called "Never Let Me Go."

In the same mode were two 1957 movies about defecting Russian aviatrixes. Janet Leigh fell into the arms of John Wayne (!) in "Jet Pilot," and Katharine Hepburn had a comic collision with Bob Hope in "The Iron Petticoat." It's hard to imagine two more improbable, uncombustible pairings.

Hollywood likes to use love as the great leveler of Red tape — a notion Peter Ustinov wittily translated into "Romanoff and Juliet" (1961), matchmaking the son (John Gavin) of the Russian ambassador (Akim Tamiroff) to the daughter (Sandra Dee) of the American ambassador (John Phillips). Other Red Star-crossed lovers have included Goldie Hawn and Hal Holbrook in "The Girl From Petrovka," Janet Leigh and Peter Lawford in "The Red Danube," Yul Brynner and Deborah Kerr in "The Journey," Alida Valli and Joseph Cotten in "The Third Man."

The most controversial film portrayals of Russians are, ironically, the most positive ones. They came in 1943-44 at the peak of our alliance with the Soviet Union, some of them at the urging of President Roosevelt — a confusing, defusing fact brought to light before the House Un-American Activities Committee. In its initial release, "The North Star," written by Lillian Hellman and directed by Lewis Milestone, depicted a Nazi-besieged Russian village; the revised reissue in the early '50s was trimmed 23 minutes to minimize Russian valor.

Robert Taylor always said he was forced into the pro-Soviet "Song of Russia" — a limp love-and-war saga, in which he starred as an American symphony conductor who marries a Russian pianist (Susan Peters) just when she's needed on the homefront to help her people fight the Nazis. And in "Mission to Moscow," Walter Huston advanced the pro-Russian viewpoint of the American Ambassador to Russia, Joseph E. Davies. In the film's foreword, the real Davies said the film represented "the truth as I saw it"; one thing he saw was a beatific view of Stalin. . . .

After the war, when the first big chill of the Cold War set in, Hollywood turned decidedly unfriendly toward Russians. Most of those who got to the screen in the late '40s and early '50s got there in varying shades of black, in lead-heavy dramas — like "The Iron Curtain" and "Prisoner of War." In the latter, Oscar Homolka played a smiling, sadistic Soviet adviser interrogating American POWs in Korea — Ronald Reagan among them.

Surprisingly though, some splendid Cold War comedies emerged in this period too. Prominent among them is 1961's "One Two Three," a fast and funny Ferenc Molnar farce successfully transplanted by adapter-director Billy Wilder in the shadow of the Berlin crisis. Stanley Kubrick seconded this motion with his brilliant "nuclear comedy," "Dr. Strangelove" (1964), in which the unseen Soviet premier is caught with his britches off by President Peter Sellers' hot-line call.

Then came detente, and comedy underscored the political thaw, most notably in Norman Jewison's delightful hands-across-the-water satire, "The Russians Are Coming, The Russians Are Coming" (1966). Here, homefront hysteria is triggered when a *wildly* off-course Soviet sub runs aground on a sandbar off Gloucester Island. Alan Arkin hilariously and timorously led the "invading force" from Russia and Ben Blue played our Latter-Day Paul Revere (only his horse had other ideas, all film long).

In "The Russians Are Coming," the Soviets were treated with demonstrably more sympathy than in previous American films. That same humanism informs "Gorky Park," which invites us to identify with the leading character — a Russian.

Although the content of American movies is often determined by what the major studios believe will be commercially successful, Soviet film-making is still, like television news, subject to direct ideological control by Party authorities. Soviet movies are supposed to cultivate specific pro-Soviet values and to portray the U.S.S.R. in a positive light. However, Soviet portrayals of Americans have varied dramatically over the years.

In the 1920s the emerging Soviet cinema showed an American senator venturing into Russia equipped with a photographic catalogue of "Types of Russian Bolsheviks," most of whom reflected common American negative stereotypes. The Senator, in Kuleshov's 1924 "The Extraordinary Adventures of Mr. West in the Land of the Bolsheviks," finds Russia every bit as wild and uncivilized as he expects — until representatives of the Soviet government come along and show him the real Moscow. American capitalists, however ill-intentioned, are portrayed in 1920s films as not particularly threatening. For example, a Russian young Communist schoolgirl foils the plan of both an American and a Russian profiteer to recover annulled tsarist debts in "The Adventure of Oktyabrina" (1924).

Early Soviet directors walked a thin line between parody and imitation of westerns and adventure films. In "Mr. West" the conceits of the western are mocked; Jeddi, the Senator's bodyguard, rides around Moscow with a revolver and lasso, and is duped and imprisoned all the same. But the pacing of the film, interestingly, is modeled after an American adventure movie. In 1926 Otsep and Bender released "Miss Mend," a suspenseful story of striking factory workers, a millionaire with multiple pretenders to his money, evil conspirators and kidnappers, and a plot to bring plague germs to the U.S.S.R. in a radio set. This Soviet film is not only set in America but quite explicitly imitates American film.

As Stalin consolidated his power, the importation of foreign films was sharply curtailed, and producers were directed to emphasize the ideological content of their films. From the mid-1930s to the beginning of World War II, only three foreign films were shown in the U.S.S.R.: Chaplin's "City Lights" and "Modern Times," and Renault's "Sous Les Toits de Paris." In 1934, as film became recognized as an extremely powerful — perhaps the most powerful — instrument of propaganda, a decree was issued instructing filmmakers to make movies more "accessible" to the public. Many projects now deemed inappropriate were abandoned halfway through. The major topics of films from this period were the successes of the new Soviet system, the dangers of foreign spies, and the leadership of Stalin. In Soviet films of this period, American workers are portrayed as enduring hard times, with many of them turning to communism. For example, millionaires and "capitalist-controlled union bosses" give underlings a lot of trouble in "Flag of the Nation" and "Nord-Ost."

After World War II, difficult conditions in America remained a popular topic of Soviet films. In "The Russian Question" (1948), an American journalist travels to Russia and learns that the Russians are not warmongers; his message is not welcome at home. He loses his job, his reputation, and eventually his wife and house to the financiers who insist that he change his tune. Other films from this era are even harsher, linking Americans with the Germans. In "Meeting on the Elbe" (1949), a German-American female spy cold-bloodedly betrays a handsome Russian commandant. American soldiers dance with German girls and glance curiously at the body of a black beaten by racists, tapping their feet to the music. Germans also suffer violence at the hands of Americans in these movies, but a connection is made among Americans, Germans, and jazz; all three are violent and heartless.

With the release of "Silver Dust" in 1953, this cycle of especially harsh anti-Americanism ended. Soviet cinema returned to some of its earlier (and still anti-American) themes — the oppression of blacks and Communists in the U.S., the corruption of the American court system, the

"Of all the arts, for us the most important is film."
V. I. Lenin

FILMS

113

Communists who save the day. After Stalin's death Soviet filmmakers began again to concentrate on domestic subjects, and for some time Americans and other Westerners rarely appeared in Soviet films. In the early 1960s the film "On the Same Planet" depicted Americans as nice people who could be trusted as international trading partners. And in a 1983 movie titled "Incident at Map-Grid 36–80," a U.S. nuclear submarine runs into trouble off the Soviet coast. The American commander is portrayed as cruel and reckless, willing to risk the lives of his own men and an accidental nuclear attack on the Soviet Union. The Soviets are seen as brave and selfless, and heroically save the day.

More recently, Soviet citizens have been exposed to images of the U.S. through various Hollywood films. "Kramer vs. Kramer," "Absence of Malice," and "Tootsie," for example, have all been shown in major Soviet cities.

Finding and going to movies, Soviet or foreign, is a markedly different experience in the Soviet Union. Americans are bombarded with advertisements for movies on television, in newspapers and magazines, on billboards, and even through "trailers" when they are seeing another movie. In contrast, Soviet citizens have far fewer sources of information about upcoming movies. Most Soviets hear about movies by word of mouth, or they learn about what is playing in town by watching for posters on kiosks or billboards. Few Soviet newspapers carry movie listings, and those which do contain only the film titles and places of showing. Moreover, the "mini-reviews" of movies common in American newspapers are largely absent from Soviet newspapers. American television often includes daily movie reviews on each of several news programs, with commentators often disagreeing on the merits of various films. In contrast, Soviet television offers just one such program weekly, "Kinopanorama." Not surprisingly, the interpretation of films on Kinopanorama is as closely monitored by the authorities as is the presentation of the news.

> **"Historically the American screen has reflected our own particular national perspective, mirroring the mood of the times."**
> **American movie critic**

THROUGH SOVIET EYES

Beneath the repeated headline "Tomorrow at the Movies," this typical Moscow film directory first lists movies and then, in darker type, theaters. As in the U.S., the same movie often can be seen at many theaters.

ЗАВТРА В КИНО ● ЗАВТРА В КИНО ● ЗАВТРА В КИНО ● ЗАВТРА В КИНО ●

«ПОМНИ» — Россия.
«XII ВСЕМИРНЫЙ. СТРАНИЦЫ ФЕСТИВАЛЬНОГО ДНЕВНИКА» — Энтузиаст.
«ЗА ВЗЛЕТОМ — ВЗЛЕТ» — Новороссийск.
«БИТВА ЗА МОСКВУ». Фильм 1-й — «АГРЕССИЯ» (2 серии) — Солнцево.
«БИТВА ЗА МОСКВУ». Фильм 2-й — «ТАЙФУН» (2 серии) — Октябрь.
«БЕРЕГА В ТУМАНЕ..» (2 серии) — Октябрь, Россия.
«ИДИ И СМОТРИ» (2 серии) — Авангард, Алмаз, Алтай, Арктика, Ба-

ку, Буревестник, Витязь, Высота, Ленинград, Одесса, Урал, Форум, Центральный детский кинотеатр.
«РЕЙС 222» (2 серии) — Ангара, Будапешт, Комсомолец, Красная Пресня, Метеор, Минск, Новатор, Патриот, Прогресс, Рубин, Сатурн, Слава, Спорт, Украина, Черемушки, Янтарь.
«ДВОЙНОЙ КАПКАН» (2 серии) — Ашхабад, Байкал, Байконур, Балтика, Варшава, Горизонт, Ереван, Зарядье, Звездный, Зенит, Казахстан, Керчь, Киргизия, Космос,

Кунцево, Москва, Имени Моссовета, Новороссийск, Первомайский, Перекоп, Правда, Прага, Саяны, София, Таджикистан, Ташкент, Тбилиси, Ударник, Ханой, Эльбрус, Эра.
«ПАРОЛЬ ЗНАЛИ ДВОЕ» — Восход, Литва, Полярный, Призыв, Свобода, Солнцево.
«САМАЯ ОБАЯТЕЛЬНАЯ И ПРИВЛЕКАТЕЛЬНАЯ» — Владивосток, Красная Пресня, Ладога, Мечта, Молодежный, Нева, Орбита, Рассвет, Рига, Севастополь, Стрела, Улан-Батор.
«СТАРШАЯ СЕСТРА». Россия.

ПРОГРАММА ПАНОРАМНЫХ ФИЛЬМОВ — Круговая кинопанорама на ВДНХ.
ПРОГРАММЫ ДОКУМЕНТАЛЬНЫХ И НАУЧНО-ПОПУЛЯРНЫХ ФИЛЬМОВ В КИНОТЕАТРАХ: Россия (Малый зал), Новороссийск, Стрела, Энтузиаст; Россия (Зал хроники) — непрерывный показ.
ПРОГРАММЫ МУЛЬТИПЛИКАЦИОННЫХ ФИЛЬМОВ В КИНОТЕАТРАХ: Россия (Малый зал), Баррикады, Орленок, Салют.

Moscow has some 113 different movie theaters. Movies are usually shown twice a day; matinees cost 25 kopeks (about 30 cents), and the evening show is priced between 30 and 70 kopeks. Features are often preceded by the showing of various newsreels, as they were in most American theaters until the early 1950s. These newsreels usually discuss industrial production, agricultural development, and other subjects of little interest to most Soviet people. Cartoons are also sometimes shown before Soviet movies. Popcorn and soft drinks, the classic American movie food, are not sold in Soviet theaters. Eating or drinking at the movies is considered uncouth.

Although foreign films make up a significant portion of Soviet moviegoers' diet and American westerns such as "The Magnificent Seven" with Yul Brynner are wildly popular, Soviet party officials determine which foreign films will be shown. American movies are usually given brief runs at a limited number of theaters. Soviet audiences nonetheless see more American movies than we see Soviet movies. The skepticism with which American film distributors approach the possibility of Soviet films' being commercially successful limits our opportunities to see such movies. One Soviet film that overcame bureaucratic obstacles in the Soviet Union and met commercial requirements in the U.S. is "Moscow Does Not Believe in Tears," winner of the 1980 Academy Award for best foreign-language film. A review of this film follows.

When the Soviet Union manifests some pride in one of its motion pictures, well, we all know what that means, right?

What it will be, this movie, is a none too subtle ode to the joys of communism, probably featuring a mannish-looking female tractor driver who, when she is not effusively thanking the government for its generosity, will likely be railing against "capitalist dogs," or whatever.

And it being a Soviet movie, it won't take more than seven or eight hours to get the message across. Right?

Well, the latest exhibit at hand is "Moscow Does Not Believe in Tears," winner of last year's Academy Award for best foreign-language film. Delightfully enough, it's not only distracting to wait for the other ideological shoe to drop in this movie, but it's also fruitless. The only barbs tossed at any government . . . are aimed at the Soviets. Very gently, to be sure, but also very real.

Ideology, in fact, has very little place in this charming romantic comedy. What it deals with instead are universal problems, particularly *the* universal problem — man-woman relationships. And it does so with warmth and wit.

The focal point of the story is the effort of three disparate women, roommates in a workers' dormitory in Moscow, to find romance and, in the finding, to better their rather tedious lives. And contained in this

Bill Hagen, "Surprise: A Good Soviet Film," *San Diego Tribune,* July 21, 1981.

effort is a surprisingly understated case for equal rights for women.

One of the women will marry her longtime sweetheart, a decent, honest, hard-working sort — maybe even a little dull — and go about raising a family. The second, who is flighty enough to be an American, will dream grandiose dreams of the good life, flirt outrageously with any man who might be able to provide it, and marry unwisely. But her spirit will never dim. She'll just keep trying in her own bubbly way.

The catalyst, however, is the third woman, a factory worker possessed of uncommon intelligence and skill but still naive and innocent enough to be seduced by a slick and very shallow television cameraman and left with a daughter to fend for herself.

And, over the years, she fends very well, indeed, eventually becoming director of the factory. Very successful, but also very unfulfilled. Until, in a delicious instance of serendipity, she meets a brash stranger on a train. It's their love story that is the bulk of "Moscow Does Not Believe in Tears," and it's a lovely story rich with insights into such phenomena as the male ego and the female heart.

With a little help from her friends — there's also a theme of enduring friendship running through this film — she's able to resolve the romance happily, but only after a few scares. It's a very human romance, filled with peaks and valleys and many marvelous moments. It's captivating, is what it is.

Whether "Moscow Does Not Believe in Tears" is a harbinger of a new direction in Soviet film making is impossible to say, given that nation's track record. It is not exactly renowned as a bastion of free expression or of artistic freedom.

And perhaps that knowledge, together with a truly charming story and outstanding acting, is what makes the film so pleasantly surprising.

Winner of the 1980 Academy Award for best foreign-language film, "Moscow Does Not Believe in Tears" is one of the few recent Soviet films to be widely seen and acclaimed by American film critics and movegoers.

Courtesy of AFI Stills Collection.

It's about women — and, almost secondarily, men — who happen to live in Moscow, but they could just as easily live in any major city in the United States. Their problems are much the same. So are their joys.

Soviet and American reviews of the same film give us a unique opportunity to compare the perceptions we hold of each other. Francis Ford Coppola's "The Outsiders" is reviewed first by Vincent Canby and then by M. Levitin.

The Outsiders" means to be about the world as it appears to its teen-agers, kids who are orphans or whose parents have abandoned them. It's about two opposing social groups, the poor boys who live on the wrong side of the Tulsa tracks and defiantly call themselves "greasers," after the foreign substance on their hair, and the "socs," pronounced "soshes," the rich society kids who live in big white houses on hills.

More specifically, it's about three "greasers." They are Ponyboy Curtis (C. Thomas Howell), whose parents are dead and who's being raised by his older brother; Johnny Cade (Ralph Macchio), a hysterical Sal Mineo type, who can't go home because his parents are such drunken slobs, and Dallas Winston (Matt Dillon), who plays a James Dean role with more early Marlon Brando mannerisms than Dean ever thought of using.

In the course of "The Outsiders," one of the "socs" is accidentally knifed to death by a "greaser," forcing Ponyboy and Johnny to go into hiding in an abandoned church in the country. There, among other things, they eat baloney sandwiches, read "Gone with the Wind" out loud, consider the manifold meanings of a "pome" by Robert Frost about sunsets and discuss the possibility of finding an ideal world without either "greasers" or "socs." In "West Side Story" that was a song called "Somewhere."

With the help of Dallas, they also become heroes by saving a bunch of schoolchildren who, when the boys are away temporarily, wander into the abandoned church which mysteriously bursts into flame. Don't ask me to make sense of this, I'm just reporting the facts.

The film ends with a climactic rumble between the "greasers" and the "socs" that settles old scores and — I think — helps Ponyboy grow up.

Vincent Canby, review of "The Outsiders," *The New York Times,* March 25, 1983.

Coppola, one of the leading directors of the contemporary American cinema, is thinking about the uselessness of fights, violence, and cruelty, about the beauty of peace, never fully revealed to the young heroes of "The Outsiders." This is the subject of his film, where in general no one is right or wrong, for everyone is guilty. But this pacifist call for social peace, with its generous share of senti-

M. Levitin, review of "The Outsiders," *Literaturnaya Gazeta* (Literary Gazette), July 13, 1983.

mentalism, this far-fetched and fundamentally questionable starry-eyed idealism in "The Outsiders" stand in palpable contradiction to the artist's sober look at the reality of America where there are not only stars, flowers and blue sky, but also poverty, unfairness and cruelty, to his active hostility to evil and his own effort — through his films — to battle this evil.

As the earlier article, "Seeing Red: How Hollywood Movies Handle the Russians," suggested, Soviet and particularly American filmmakers' portrayals of each other's countries have worsened lately. American studios in the mid-1980s produced a spate of movies depicting the Soviets as hostile and evil. The following articles, one from the *The New York Times* and one from *Izvestia,* describe a Soviet response to these movies.

"Soviet Pans 'Rocky' and 'Rambo' Films," *New York Times,* January 4, 1986.

A group of Soviet cultural officials and artists today denounced the movies "Rocky IV" and "Rambo: First Blood, Part II" as part of a deliberate propaganda campaign to portray Russians as cruel and treacherous enemies.

Sitting behind the same table in the Foreign Ministry press center where Soviet spokesmen usually condemn United States Government policies, the group — including the poet Yevgeny Yevtushenko —

Despite short theater runs and minimal publicity, screenings of Western movies such as "Kramer vs. Kramer" are generally sold out at Moscow theaters.

Bettman Archive.

singled out the two popular movies starring Sylvester Stallone as representative of what they called a rash of anti-Soviet propaganda in American movies and on television.

In "Rambo: First Blood, Part II," Mr. Stallone plays an anti-Communist Vietnam veteran who returns to Southeast Asia to try to rescue American prisoners, killing more than a dozen Russians in the process. In "Rocky IV," as prizefighter Rocky Balboa, he battles a villainous Soviet boxer.

Georgi A. Ivanov, a Deputy Minister of Culture, told a news conference that American films are "pushing onto the screens a new type of hero, a killer with ideological convictions."

KILLING WITH 'PERVERSE RELISH'

This new hero, he went on, "kills 'Reds' and Russians not for money but with a kind of perverse relish." Such fare, he said, was part of "an anti-Soviet campaign mounted in the United States."

The announced subject of the news conference was the resumption of American-Soviet cultural exchanges, but the panel devoted much of the 90-minute briefing to criticizing American films.

Mr. Yevtushenko, who created a stir at a congress of Soviet writers recently when he called for an end to censorship in Soviet literature, described movies like Mr. Stallone's as a form of pornography.

"I call them war-nography," Mr. Yevtushenko said.

Genrikh Borovik, a secretary of the Soviet Writers' Union, said Hollywood was "using art to sell hatred and fear."

Mr. Borovik also cited the movie "Red Dawn" as another example of virulent anti-Soviet propaganda.

The "Spirit of Geneva," which arose as a result of the Soviet-American summit meeting, has brought a glimmer of hope to people who live in fear of a nuclear missile catastrophe. . . . [Unfortunately], opponents of the positive developments of Soviet-American relations are poisoning them not only by erecting barriers to genuine art, but also by opening the floodgates to anti-art. Reactionary U.S. circles, especially in recent times, have been subjecting the American public to an intensive ideological barrage, instilling anti-Soviet moods and sowing hatred for our people and our state. To illustrate the point, it is enough to mention such film hits as "Red Dawn," "Invasion USA," "Rambo: First Blood, Part II" and "Rocky IV." Or, for example, "Amerika," a film planned by the American NBC [sic] television network [*Ed. note:* the film is planned by ABC]. In content (if one may call it that) the TV film, which stretches over 16 hours, portrays a ravaged America gripped by fear, under "Red" occupation for the fifth decade! As the *Los Angeles Times* admits in this connection, anti-Soviet paranoia "has recently taken new forms, reflecting even more reaction-

"The Spirit of Geneva and Culture," *Izvestia*, January 13, 1986.

ary moods than those that were observed in America in the 1950s, in the days of McCarthyism. . . ."

I am in complete agreement with my colleague from the *New York Times Magazine*, who recently wrote: "If the Russians began making films about the seizure of the Soviet Union by the United States, we could rightly accuse them of whipping up hysteria and hatred toward Americans and of increasing international tension. And we would have some grounds for fearing the impact on the U.S.S.R.'s population, just as we now have reason to be alarmed about the impact of this 'entertainment' on Americans."

Anti-art and anti-culture contribute to a dangerous increase in the lack of trust. . . .

Some Americans feel that the Soviets, with their government-controlled film industry, have no business critizing whatever Hollywood studios choose to produce. This view is reflected in the following *Washington Post* editorial.

"Red Pan," *Washington Post,* editorial, July 7, 1986.

One of the more bizarre "cultural exchanges" on Soviet-American record took place in Moscow the other day. Out trotted a deputy minister of culture and favored gadfly, Yevgeny Yevtushenko, to declare that some recent American films have a crude, harmful and officially inspired anti-Soviet theme. The pan dominated a press conference nominally called to tell about the Soviet dancers and others scheduled to visit the United States this year in the post-Geneva-summit thaw.

Others will have to disentangle the mesh of innocent misunderstanding and willful deception in the Soviet complaint. We will merely note that the Kremlin is without standing to join the debate already in progress in the United States on the likes of the "Rocky" and "Rambo" films and, for that matter, on every other film and television series that gets made here. A totalitarian government that defines orthodoxy, punishes unorthodoxy, peddles untruth and cant at will and renders all literary output official cannot pretend that a free government is similarly responsible for its society's creative flow.

Movies and other products of the popular culture do, of course, relate to the political culture. The influences that have turned American politics rightward in recent years have inevitably found expression in film. But those influences start not with a secret cable from Washington to Hollywood but with real events, such as the Soviet invasion of Afghanistan and the repression of Andrei Sakharov.

Not so incidentally, this sensitivity to real life is a leading reason why American movies are interesting — even when they're bad. Insensitivity to real life is why Soviet movies are dull. Such insensitivity is also why the American films in question, although unavailable to the Soviet public, are much prized by the elite with access to them — including no doubt the people who gave the press conference: not for any anti-Soviet quality but for the very elements of drama, imagination and raw life that draw American audiences.

There is a raw anti-Soviet message in some of these films. They have been criticized by some Americans for their anti-Sovietism and for their rawness alike. The message, however, is only one of many political and cultural messages bouncing around freely in American society at any given time. On this matter, in any event, Americans need no prodding from spokesmen for a government that deals with its independent-minded creators in ways of which criticism is the mildest.

In response to this editorial, the director of the U.S.-U.S.S.R. Project for the American Friends Service Committee wrote the following unpublished essay.

"Reactionary U.S. circles . . . have been subjecting the American public to an intensive ideological barrage."
Izvestia

I n its editorial of January 7, "Red Pan," the *Post* took the position that the Soviet Union has no right to complain of the recent rash of anti-Soviet films in the U.S., because all the arts in the U.S.S.R. are censored and the Soviet film industry is government-controlled. It is true that the film industries are, like virtually every industry in the Soviet Union, State-owned, rather than private entities. It is also true that the Soviets probably view the American situation from their own experience and may believe the U.S. government could, if it chose, discourage the production of such films as "Rambo," "Rocky IV," and "Red Dawn."

Sylvia Eastman, "Soviet Films: More Than Propaganda," January 25, 1986.

But the editorial doesn't stop there. It insists that Soviet films are "dull" because of "insensitivity to real life," and David Remnick (January 12, "Reds Nix Sly's Pix") claims the Soviet government "doesn't have the guts to produce anything but 'agitational propaganda' . . . art."

If you want "real life," you're more likely to find it in a Soviet film than from Hollywood. The editorial claims that it is the "very elements of drama, imagination and raw life that draw American audiences." If you want drama, I suggest you see "Without Witness," "A Wartime Romance," "The Dawns Are Quiet Here." And for raw life, I dare you to try "Come and See."

I admire contemporary Soviet films for many reasons. First, they are works of art. Photography, script, direction, acting, set and costume design are all strikingly impressive in the vast majority of films I've seen. "An Unfinished Piece for Player Piano," "A Wartime Romance," and "Kalina Krasnaya" present scenes of breathtaking beauty.

Then there is stark realism, the portrayal of life and people with all their blemishes. Soviet film stars are frequently older and plainer than ours and do not possess the glamor and tinsel of Hollywood. They may even appear rather unsympathetic characters when we at first see their

IT'S AN AMERICAN SET...
YOUR SIXTEEN CHESS
PIECES VERSUS
RAMBO

Neil, *The Bulletin* (Sydney, Australia), reprinted in *World Press Review.*

many failings, yet superb acting makes them both real and beautiful. Note "Kalina Krasnaya," "A Time of Desires," "Without Witness," "Waiting for Love," and "Moscow Does Not Believe in Tears."

Many Soviet films demonstrate a surprising degree of artistic freedom — they may illustrate the weaknesses and failings of the communist system and poke fun at what is wrong about Soviet society. I am not suggesting that censorship doesn't exist or that there are not many forbidden subjects. I think, however, few Americans would fail to be surprised at some of the things that occur in Soviet films. Examples abound: "Jazzman" laughs at stuffy bureaucrats who try to censor art; "Moscow Does Not Believe in Tears" and so many other films make perpetual jokes at the inconveniences and inequities of life in the Soviet Union. Nonconformists are frequently the surprise heroes and heroines — in "Flights of Fancy, Awake and in Dreams," "Two for the Railway Station," "Kalina Krasnaya." "The Blond Around the Corner" depicts the underground economy with its theft, barter, and black market. The blonde who practices this anti-socialist behavior is not depicted as the scourge of society, but as a humorous and lovable heroine of sorts.

A cartoon short seen in Moscow a couple of summers ago showed the fairy godmother changing Cinderella's rags into an elegant gown. A department store manager, watching, asked, "Could you do that with the drab dresses in my store?" and the fairy godmother changed them into the latest fashions. Suddenly, these fashionable clothes disappeared, and even the fairy godmother didn't know what had happened to them. She asked the store manager, who said, "Simple — any time we get some decent merchandise in the store, it disappears under the counter."

Most pertinent to the issue of films that glorify war and violence and demonize the supposed "enemy" is Soviet treatment of the same subject. Unlike most American civilians, the Soviet people know what war is. Whether in literature or film, war is depicted as abhorrent. Consider the pacifist messages in "The Dawns Are Quiet Here," "The Cranes Are

Flying," and the poignant "Ballad of a Soldier."

Nothing Hollywood has yet conceived can compare with the "raw life" in an unbearable, yet most important movie, the 1985 Moscow film festival's gold prize winner, "Come and See." Its realistic portrayal of how innocent civilians suffer during war is so painful one can barely endure it. Although bestial acts of Nazi soldiers are vividly portrayed, the closing sequence recognizes there is a common humanity in us all. Blind hatred of one's enemy only perpetuates the cycle of violence — a cycle that can be interrupted by compassion and forgiveness.

The real question in comparing American and Soviet films is how each nation's art and culture reflect its values, and whether they honor truth and promote human understanding, peace, and justice. This is not a plea for censorship. It is a plea for recognition that the Soviets have something of value to offer. Dehumanizing one another only makes it easier to contemplate mutual annihilation — it does not bring us closer to resolving our differences.

Yet another dimension of the debate within America, within the Soviet Union, and between Soviets and Americans over the quality of Soviet and American films is explored in the following article by an American Sovietologist.

The Soviet Union has been complaining about a number of American films dealing with the Soviet Union, and recently there have, in fact, been quite a few of them: "Red Dawn," "Rambo," "Rocky IV," "White Nights," and "Spies Like Us." Clearly these movies have been touching something in the minds of the young American audience, and we, like the Soviets, should ask what it is.

Jerry Hough, "Rocky, Rambo, and the American Mood," *Christian Science Monitor*, February 24, 1986.

Without question, these films do contain deeply anti-Soviet scenes that rightly offend the Soviets — and that should shame Americans. And yet, if one looks at these films as a whole and tries to understand their overall themes, they create a very strange impression.

In "Red Dawn," the Soviets are strong enough to capture Colorado, but not strong enough to cope with eight high school students. In "White Nights," the KGB is painted in very black terms, but at the end it gives in to third-world public opinion. (And the main memory from the film is the great beauty of Leningrad.) In "Rocky IV," the Soviet crowd at the fight, with the Politburo watching, roots for Rocky against Drago in the closing rounds.

Moreover, "Rambo" and "Rocky IV," unlike "Star Wars," are extremely negative about technology and do nothing to glorify the present military buildup. (And in "Red Dawn," it doesn't even prevent a takeover of Colorado.) "Rambo" ends with the hero destroying a large American computer with his machine gun. "Rocky IV" has long scenes in which the Russian is trained with high technology, while Rocky has a simple, peasantlike training program. And American backwardness defeats the high-technology Russians! One almost suspects Stallone of being a KGB plant with the mission of destroying faith in President Reagan's SDI program.

There is no ambiguity at all about the lesson of "Spies Like Us." The American military sends spies to the Soviet Union to capture and launch a Soviet missile so that the American space defense can shoot it down. The space defense fails, and the American military does not tell the President why a Soviet missile is coming in, for they are indifferent to nuclear holocaust. This is strong stuff. Only cooperation between simple Russians and simple Americans saves the world at the end.

In its own way, each of these films is conveying the message that Russians are not 10 feet tall, that they are not an insuperable threat. This is the same theme of the many [television] commercials with a Russian theme, all of which belittle the Soviet Union rather than treat it as threatening. We clearly need a middle ground between the image of a Soviet totalitarian juggernaut of the past and the image of an impotent Soviet Union of today, but the popularity of the films and commercials is saying that the sense of threat that drove the United States in the late 1970s is disappearing.

Indeed, except in "Rambo," the Russians somehow become more sympathetic at the end. "Rocky IV" carries this to its ultimate conclusion. The old Russian menace in the person of Drago is inhuman, and it is totally committed to victory. At the beginning of the fight, the Western commentator says that Drago is "a man with an entire country in his corner." By Round 12, however, the Russian boos for Rocky have turned to cheers. Drago represents what has been terrible in Russia, and the Russians are cheering for its defeat.

After his victory, Rocky drives the point home. He tells the Russian crowd: "When I came here I didn't know what to expect. All I seen is a lotta people hating me and I guess I didn't like you too much neither. During this fight I seen a lot of changing in the way youse felt about me and the way I felt about you. . . . If I can change and you can change, everybody can change." Mikhail Gorbachev, who had been watching suspiciously, rose and applauded vigorously. The Politburo followed.

The United States is in transition. The 25-year-old moviegoer was born in 1960, the 15-year-old in 1970. Their parents were members of the Eisenhower and Vietnam generations, respectively, and passed on very different values to their children. Moviemakers have to mix their themes to appeal to a diverse audience, but they know which audience is passing out of the theaters.

For all these reasons, the Soviets should not get so uptight about what these films show about the American mind. They should take "Rocky IV" to heart. There has been an alien, Drago-like character to the Soviet posture in the past, and Russians should applaud its defeat. Even Rocky is willing to meet the new Russians halfway.

How should we, as an open society, respond to recent complaints about what the Soviets view as offensive, anti-Soviet, American-made movies?

If American filmmakers are currently portraying Soviets as sometimes demonic, sometimes laughable, how are Soviet filmmakers portraying Americans? Most current Soviet movies focus on fictional or domestic themes. For example, the January 1986 issue of *Soviet Film* announced several new movies: "Extraterrestrial Ship," a space science-fiction movie; "Estonian Documentaries," about the Soviet Republic of Estonia; "Fronting the Arctic," about nature and life in the far north; "Winter Cherry," a psychological portrait of the modern woman; "The Third Generation," about economic development and conservation in the Far East; "Who Will Correct Demeter's Error?," about environmental problems; and "Sniper Liya," on the ever-present subject of World War II.

Only one new movie described in *Soviet Film*, "Coordinates of Death," involves images of America. A description of the movie follows.

The Central Gorky Studios of Children's and Youth Films has completed this picture set in Vietnam in the early 1970s.

Ilya Krutin (played by Alexander Galibin), a Soviet civil engineer, having arrived in Vietnam, becomes an eyewitness of the war waged by the U.S. aggressive circles. He is caught up in dramatic events. An American mine is to be defused and they need a volunteer to do it. Ilya Krutin, who happens to be present at the meeting, offers his help.

Thousands of such U.S. mines were used to block the port of Haiphong, preventing foreign ships from unloading food, building materials and other vital cargoes. Krutin and Vietnamese sapper [sic] Vong managed to defuse the deadly mine.

Today we know who won that war. We know the trials and suffering the courageous people of Vietnam endured in order to be able to smile again. "The Coordinates of Death" is a tribute to the heroic and unconquered nation fighting for its freedom and reunification, and about the fraternal help of the Soviet Union and other countries. It was a stern and dramatic period as the title of the film suggests. The directors are Samvel Gasparov and Nguyen Suan Tian.

Samvel Gasparov:

"The screenplay was written by Alexander Lapshin, U.S.S.R. prizewinner, jointly with Hoang Tit-Ti, a Vietnamese dramatist. This is the first Soviet-Vietnamese co-production. I think both sides are pleased with their cooperation. The entire film, with the exception of a single episode, was shot in Vietnam where we spent three months working in Ho Chi Minh, Hanoi, Haiphong, and in the jungle where arms and food supplies for the People's Army were delivered during the war. We got to know Vietnam and its wonderful people very well.

"The cast includes Alexander Galibin, Yuri Nazarov, Tatiana Lebedeva, Viet Bao, and Le Wan. I think our actors, especially the young ones, benefited a lot from communicating with their peers from Vietnam who have experienced all

Tatiana Sanina, review of "Coordinates of Death," *Soviet Film*, January 1986.

the horror of war early on in their lives. Working on the film about Vietnamese heroism and patriotism we learnt a great deal. And the great value of peace on earth was brought home to us. Our film is about war but it is against war, for a life without smouldering ruins and gun fire."

Although the tone of specific movies being produced has tended to fluctuate in predictable ways with the political climate, new technology now presents a complex challenge (and opportunity?) for the Soviet government. As in America, the popularity of video cassette recorders (VCRs) makes it possible for Soviet citizens to play and watch movies on their own schedules. VCRs are still a rare and precious possession in the Soviet Union (produced by the thousands, in contrast to the millions sold each year in the U.S.), but their availability is growing. Roughly two dozen cassette-rental outlets have opened in the U.S.S.R. since 1985. The supply of approved movies for rent is augmented by a regular flow of forbidden foreign movies available on the black market.

Because video cassettes can be viewed in the privacy of the home and because they can be copied with relative ease, their potential as a source of alternative information and perceptions is tremendous. The following article describes the growth of VCRs in the Soviet Union from an American perspective. Next is an article from a Soviet magazine, *Nedelya*.

"Oh Comrade, Can I Borrow Your Rambo Cassette?," *The New York Times*, December 9, 1985.

The Russian host, a nonconformist writer, flipped on his television, slipped a cassette into the Japanese video player and pressed the play button.

The first frames of "The Good, the Bad and the Ugly," an early Clint Eastwood Western, flickered on the screen.

"These opening scenes are great," the host said with anticipatory pleasure as he settled into an armchair.

Video recorders, which made their entry on the Soviet scene in the late 1970s as novelties that only the elite could find or afford, have started to become a mass phenomenon.

MOST FILMS MADE IN WEST

Although the number of owners remains far smaller and the cost is still far higher than in the West, increasing numbers of Russians are watching movies at home, according to newspaper reports and Muscovites.

Most of the films they watch were made in the West and are officially banned in the Soviet Union, the Russians said.

The growth in video usage has forced the Government to rethink its initial response to video players — a heavy-handed effort to prevent their introduction and discourage their use.

Apparently persuaded that this approach only forced the business

underground, the Government is now trying to control the trade by embracing it.

In recent months the Soviet Union has started mass-producing video players, made available a limited but growing selection of ideologically safe films, and opened video stores that, like their counterparts in the United States, rent movies overnight.

Despite the efforts, the Soviet authorities have had a hard time keeping home video viewing within acceptable political limits. Pornographic films, which were popular when video recorders made their debut, have been supplanted by more serious movies that pose a greater threat to political orthodoxy.

One of the most popular movies in Moscow this fall, according to Russians, has been "Man of Iron," a Polish film by the director Andrzej Wajda that sympathetically chronicles labor unrest in Gdansk, the birthplace of the Solidarity labor union movement.

The films of Ingmar Bergman, Federico Fellini, Milos Forman and Bernardo Bertolucci circulate widely in Moscow, often in copies that bear English subtitles but are also dubbed in Russian. "Amadeus," Mr. Forman's Academy Award-winning movie about Mozart and Antonio Salieri, is among the hottest video properties in the capital, according to Muscovites.

"AMERIKA"

In early 1986 a controversy erupted when the Soviet Union strenuously objected to a proposed ABC movie, "Amerika," arguing that it would damage chances for improved relations. What follows is the full ABC statement relating to this controversy.

Brandon Stoddard, President of ABC Entertainment, has announced that ABC Circle Films will begin production of the 12-hour miniseries, "Amerika," for broadcast on the ABC Television Network during the spring of 1987.

Mr. Stoddard said, "In light of the inherent dramatic quality of the material, the decision to present 'Amerika' was an easy one.

"'Amerika' is a powerful program about freedom and responsibility and the American character," Mr. Stoddard said. "There is no doubt in my mind that this program will continue the tradition of thoughtful, important dramatic productions that we have presented over the years through our 'ABC Theater' and 'ABC Novels for Television' presentations."

Despite inaccurate reports that ABC had cancelled "Amerika," Mr. Stoddard emphasized that the project was briefly postponed pending a final budget evaluation, but he added, "There was never any lack of our faith in the concept of the script for 'Amerika.'"

John B. Sias, President of ABC Television, said: "We decided to go ahead with 'Amerika' because we believe in the project. I think it will be a program in the tradition of 'Roots,' 'The Winds of War,' 'The Day After' and 'Massada.' I also think it should be made clear that this decision was made by our entertainment division, supported by top management and with the full understanding of what pressures this decision might bring to other areas of our company."

"Amerika" deals with contemporary American life 10 years after a takeover by the Soviet Union. It is an original drama by Donald Wrye who will also serve as executive producer and director on the project.

Older films like Mr. Bertolucci's "Last Tango in Paris" and Mr. Bergman's "Fanny and Alexander" are very popular, Muscovites said.

MOSCOW YEARNS FOR STALLONE

Sylvester Stallone's first "Rambo" movie has attracted a large following. Video owners said they were eager to see "Rambo: First Blood Part II," one of Mr. Stallone's later features.

In many ways, the video business remains a primitive and costly one compared with the business in the West. The going rate for having a movie dubbed into Russian is about 30 rubles. A ruble is $1.28 at the official exchange rate, and the average Soviet worker earns about 190 rubles a month.

But Russians said this was a vast improvement over the first efforts to translate films, which involved hiring someone to do a simultaneous translation while a movie was shown.

Blank tapes are particularly expensive. A tape that costs $5 in the United States sells for the equivalent of between $60 and $70 on the black market in Moscow.

Prices, however, have fallen in recent years as the availability of video players and movies has increased. Japanese and other foreign-made video players sell for about 2,500 rubles in Moscow at "commission stores," second-hand goods outlets run by the Government. Two years ago the cost in Moscow was 3,500 rubles.

Copies of Western movies, available only on the black market, may sell for 200 or 250 rubles in Moscow. Western movies are brought into the country by tourists, by Russians who travel abroad, and by some diplomats, whose luggage is not checked at customs.

NOT COMPATIBLE WITH WEST'S

Soviet video players and television sets are not compatible with American, Japanese or most Western European models. The Soviet equipment, however, can be converted to handle movies recorded for other video systems, and a prospering underground business has developed to do just that, according to Muscovites. They said it costs about 400 rubles to have a Soviet color television converted.

The Soviet video player, the Elektronika VM, costs 1,200 rubles. In October, as part of a new drive to increase the availability of consumer goods, the Government announced that it planned to produce 60,000 video players a year by 1990 and 120,000 a year by 2000.

By Western standards, the goal was small. Millions of video players are sold every year in the United States. But for the Soviet Union, the totals were considered less important that the fact that the Government had decided to mass-produce a product that until recently it considered decadent and politically dangerous.

There are no official figures available for the number of video players sold annually in past years or the number of households with video machines.

The first video rental store, called a Videoteka, opened in May in Voronezh, a city about 300 miles south of Moscow. Since then other outlets have opened around the Soviet Union.

There are two rental outlets in Moscow. One is in the basement of a movie theater near the central farmer's market. The decor is drab, and, unlike American video stores, there are no cassette covers lined up along the wall to advertise the selection of movies. Andrei G. Tkachenko, a salesman, said the store has a library of 270 films.

The movies, all of which were made in the Soviet Union or the Soviet

How would we react to advance publicity for a Soviet movie depicting a U.S. invasion of Eastern Europe?

bloc, with the exception of a few made in India, range from historical epics such as Sergei Eisenstein's "Ivan the Terrible" to current comedies and children's films.

The movies rent for two or three rubles a day.

Arsen Kuchuberiya, an auto mechanic, stopped in on a recent afternoon with his wife. They rented a detective movie called "The Pub on Pyatnitskaya Street" and "Scarecrow," a popular Russian film about the cruelties that schoolchildren inflict on a classmate they believe has betrayed them.

Mr. Kuchuberiya said he stops at the store four times a week on his way to work.

"I dreamed of buying a video player for years and we refrained from getting other things we wanted so we could afford one," Mr. Kuchuberiya said. He said he spent 3,000 rubles for a Japanese video player 18 months ago.

Mr. Tkachenko said about 50 customers visit the store every day.

Yevgeny K. Voitovich, the head of the film rental program, which is operated under the auspices of the State Committee for Cinematography, said in a recent newspaper article that the home video market was in danger of being "seized by uncontrollable foreign films."

In an effort to control the supply of films, Mr. Voitovich said, the committee will soon begin offering some Western films for rental and will also offer language instruction and exercise cassettes.

But the allure of forbidden Western movies will be difficult to blunt. One Muscovite, a man who holds a senior academic post, said he watches several foreign films a week at home.

"These films have helped me and my friends understand life in the West," he said.

"What Future for Videotapes in the USSR?," *Nedelya,* in *The Current Digest of the Soviet Press,* vol. XXXVII, no. 36, 1985, p. 10.

Video Library: Video Today and Tomorrow: What's Holding Things Up?" (*Nedelya,* Aug. 12–18, p. 18. 1,900 words. Condensed text.) *Prognosis* (By Candidate of Art History Aleksandr Lipkov). . . . The acquisition of videotape recorders (at considerable price) is still a major problem: The Soviet-made machines are sold for use with tape that was produced who knows when and will be produced again who knows when; as for the imported machines, you have to be very crafty and get hold of one however you can. Indeed, psychologically speaking, the sizable number of articles about all sorts of shady "video affairs" involving underground speculation in cassettes and the showing of "indecent" films brought in from "over there" predispose the future owner of a video system to regard it, if not as something downright criminal, then certainly as something that is reprehensible and antisocial. . . .

We have now grown accustomed to the fact that television, by its very nature, is aimed at communicating with the individual. But let's re-

> If Americans see VCRs as a challenge to Soviet control of information, how are Soviets likely to see the influence of VCRs on American life?

Posters in Tallin, the capital of the Soviet Republic of Estonia, advertise films in Russian and Estonian: "No Place for Strangers" and "An Unscheduled Train."
Courtesy of Betty Ann J. Halperin.

member that it began as a collective medium. The lucky owners of KVNs [early Soviet television sets — *Trans.*] . . . became . . . the proprietors of small "TV theaters," where friends and neighbors gathered and watched together.

Today the owners of videos find themselves in roughly the same situation. And, until the demand for video equipment is fully satisfied, it will not change. Therefore, it is appropriate to turn our attention first of all to collective forms of the use of videotape recorders. . . .

The schools should be equipped with them. The schools first of all. . . .

Recordings on magnetic tape will give an impetus to new forms of amateur filmmaking. The portable television camera will become the tourist's companion. . . .

We are not forgetting, either, that no matter how far-flung our film-distribution network is, there are "empty spots" in it. In many instances (in villages with a small number of inhabitants, for example), a club's videotape recorder can be more effective. . . . At the same time, it will give a better quality picture: We know what condition filmprints are in when they arrive in the "boondocks."

And let's not forget about the "empty spots" on the map of television reception — there, the video cassette is simply indispensable. All this makes the question of what will be recorded on the cassettes an especially urgent point on the agenda. . . .

Only one little thing is lacking — a spirit of enterprise on our part, a spirit of initiative. Meanwhile, the development rate of video equipment and video service in our country has fallen far behind the rate at which the uncontrolled video influx, so to speak, is growing. The only effective measure here will be our enterprisingness in organizing the video business. . . .

FILMS

131

Widely regarded as one of the most important works in the history of film, "Potemkin" by Russian director Sergei Eisenstein is the story of a mutiny in 1905 aboard the Czar's cruiser, Potemkin.

Cinemabilia.

Diagnosis. — So what about enterprisingness? . . . We addressed [this question] to Ye. K. Voitovich, Director of the U.S.S.R. State Cinematography Committee's Chief Administration for Building Movie Theaters and Distributing Films, as well as to V. G. Olitsky, head of the recently created department for the planning of videotape repertoires, the printing of copies and the organization of videotape rental under Soyuskinofond [All-Union Film Library Association].

As our conversation revealed, these are complex questions. . . . Ye. Voitovich said: "The organizations that should be vitally interested in the rapid development of the video business are apparently not yet aware of either the social role it has been assigned or the importance of the prospects that are opening up. They act as if this were a question of the distant future. . . . Correspondence went on for many months concerning premises for rental locations and a video center. We inspected a great many 'facilities' that were quite suitable, but one refusal followed another. Finally, we were assigned the former Science and Knowledge movie theater in the Arbat — it is now being outfitted with a 50-seat auditorium and facilities for the viewing and rental of video cassettes. . . .

"I want to stress," Ye. Voitovich continued, "that we cannot wait passively until our 'video market' is completely captured by an uncontrolled influx of foreign videotapes. The videotape recorder is becoming part of our everyday life, and providing it with a diverse and rich repertoire of Soviet video programs is an ideological question."

Question. — What will this repertoire be like?

V. Olitsky. — We are putting virtually the whole existing stock of Soviet films on cassettes, from the classics to the latest films. An accord has been reached with cinematographers in the socialist countries, and all the best films that we buy from them will simultaneously come to us for video distribution, too. Many films from capitalist countries will be repurchases for video cassettes — among them the works of outstanding masters of the world cinema and the best examples of genres that are popular with viewers. Some films will be acquired solely for video distribution.

But cinematic works are only a small part of the repertoire. . . . After all, a cassette can teach you how to run a household, how to renovate your apartment, how to train your dog, the proper way to do gymnastic and aerobic exercises, how to drive a car, how to swim. . . .

Today video is just beginning. Tomorrow it will be part of our everyday life. Its social role in the future will be enormous. We will grow accustomed to it.

On a topic as seemingly mundane as VCRs, and even after interviewing the same official (Ye. K. Voitovich), the tone and interpretation of the two articles are striking — both for their differences, and for their subtle similarities. The American story emphasizes the difficulties VCRs present for control in Soviet society. The opportunities for wider distribution of films and educational programs are highlighted in the Soviet article. Neither story is "right" or "wrong" — any more than it is "right" or "wrong" to eat in movie theaters. But both stories, like films themselves, contain messages just beneath their surfaces which influence how we perceive the Soviet Union.

If the American stereotype of Soviets is captured in the (imaginary) movie title "Boy Meets Tractor," what is a movie title that best reflects Soviet stereotypes of Americans?

CONCLUSION

As the preceding chapters illustrate, citizens of both the U.S. and the U.S.S.R. are bombarded with a multitude of written, verbal, and visual images of each other. Some of these images allow us to see each other in a clearer light; others are misleading. Our media sometimes ignore, misunderstand, or misinterpret Soviet developments; the Soviet media routinely present a distorted picture of American life. American schoolbooks generally ignore Soviet history, and Soviet texts stress the negative aspects of America. To ensure box-office success, Hollywood frequently falls back on stereotypes of the Soviet Union. And to meet ideological demands, Soviet movies regularly portray America harshly.

The reasons for these distortions vary markedly. Soviets and Americans are destined to live with the very different histories and experiences of our two nations. Soviet and American interpretations of history are unlikely ever to be in accord. Beneath our divergent perceptions of events are broader, deeply held cultural assumptions, and these too diverge. By understanding these fundamental views and assumptions we can begin to understand more fully how we and the Soviets interpret each others' actions and how these interpretations in turn affect those actions.

Despite such divergent interpretations and perceptions, certain underlying conditions are similar in the U.S. and the U.S.S.R. Patriotism and nationalism, for example, are powerful forces in both nations, and each government portrays the other as "the threat," an adversary to be feared and resisted.

What can we conclude? Our perceptions of each other and of ourselves are different and often contradictory. But are these perceptions really so important? Does it matter what the Soviet people think about the U.S.? Because power is held by an elite few, what difference does it make if the Soviet people see America as friend or foe?

There are no easy answers to these questions. They may, in fact, be

> **"Surely it is in our interest that the peoples in the Soviet Union should know the truth about the United States. And surely it can only enrich our lives to learn more about them."**
> **Ronald Reagan**
> **June 20, 1986**

■ **135**

Soviet map of U.S., East Coast and Midwest, courtesy of U.S.S.R. Embassy, Washington, DC.

answerable only by historians who in time look back and see us with greater clarity than we now see ourselves. We do know, however, that the roles played by perceptions in the U.S. and the U.S.S.R are clearly not the same. Elected officials in the U.S. develop policies that largely reflect their and their constituents' views. More generally, the influence of public perceptions is felt in the constant give-and-take of our democratic institutions and society. In Soviet society it is far more difficult to evaluate the importance of perceptions. Perceptions of the party elite certainly influence Soviet policies toward the U.S. And although Soviet leaders may satisfy more of their people's demands than most of us assume, they can also ignore public opinion with great impunity. They need not fear the reaction of an angry Congress or the votes of outraged citizens. Although popular support for the Soviet government plays a role in the long run, public perceptions have very little influence on day-to-day Soviet decision making.

Soviet and American society are different and will remain so even if we manage to cultivate a clearer and more realistic view of one another. Heightened understanding and awareness will not alone vanquish the obstacles that stand in the way of more stable relations between the two nations. They are only a first step — but they are a vital first step, as is eloquently stated in the final piece in this book by J. William Fulbright, former five-term U.S. Senator and Chairman of the Senate Foreign Relations Committee.

Senator J. W. Fulbright, Speech given at Duke University, September 22, 1983.

In foreign, as in personal relations, our inferences are shaped as much by how we look at a person, or a situation, as by what we actually see. There are few foreign countries of which we do not have certain preconceptions — to their good or ill intentions — and these exert a powerful influence on our evaluation of their specific acts or policies.

Some years ago, the noted philosopher-psychologist, Dr. Erich Fromm, put the matter in these words:

"The lack of objectivity, as far as foreign nations is concerned, is notorious. From one day to the next, another nation is made out to be utterly depraved and fiendish, while one's own nation stands for everything that is good and noble. Every action of the enemy is judged by one standard — every action by oneself by another. Even good deeds by the enemy are considered a sign of particular devilishness meant to deceive us and the world, while our bad deeds are necessary and justified by our noble goals which we serve."

When we ruthlessly took possession of the Philippines after the war with Spain it was to "Christianize and civilize" them, in the words of President McKinley. When Russia invaded and occupied Afghanistan, it was to subdue and exploit them. When our friend Israel shot down the Libyan civilian plane in which 108 passengers died near the Suez Canal in 1973, we showed little concern about it, but when that Russian pilot

"THE RULING CIRCLES OF THE _____* HAVE LAUNCHED POLITICAL, IDEOLOGICAL AND ECONOMIC OFFENSIVES AGAINST US AND HAVE RAISED THE INTENSITY OF THEIR MILITARY PREPARATIONS... THEY HAVE UNFOLDED AN UNPRECENTED ARMS RACE, ESPECIALLY A NUCLEAR ARMS RACE, AND ARE TRYING TO ATTAIN MILITARY SUPERIORITY!"

*Fill in the blanks: INSERT "Soviet Union" OR "United States"... THEN GUESS WHO **REALLY** SAID IT.

Courtesy of Seattle Post—Intelligencer.

shot down the Korean plane, it was an act of deliberate terrorism calling for world-wide sanctions. We should understand that the total pattern of human behavior in thought, social forms, speech, beliefs, and traditions of the Russian people is quite different from ours.

This difference in our view between two quite similar acts, one by a friendly country, the other by the Soviets, prompts me to recall the advice of perhaps the wisest President we have ever had (our first) when he said in his farewell address:

"The nation which indulges toward another an habitual hatred, or an habitual fondness, is in some degree a slave. It is a slave to its animosity or to its affection, either of which is sufficient to lead it astray from its duty and its interest." . . .

Our preconceptions about a country, or how we look at a situation, has a powerful influence upon our judgment with regard to either. The better we understand our own or our adversary's preconceptions and motives, the more likely we are to arrive at a judgment based upon reality and not upon error.

There is little if any prospect that Russia will collapse economically, that it will be torn by internal revolution or that it will voluntarily retire from the competition for influence in the third world. It is a rival great power and we must deal with it and find the means to lessen the virulence of our mutual animosity.

If we are to avoid the ultimate disaster of a major conflict with the Russians, it is imperative that we understand their value system and society which is so profoundly different from our own. Without such an understanding we will surely continue to make mistakes in judgment in dealing with them that could be disastrous. In order to understand them, we must be cognizant of their historical experiences, their government, and their culture as a whole. In a very real sense, the future of the world is hostage to the ability of the Soviets and the Americans to evaluate correctly their intentions toward each other.

READER'S GUIDE

INTRODUCTION

This Guide is a companion to *The Other Side*, the first book in a series published by the Committee for National Security and entitled *Beyond the Kremlin*. It is designed for use by a wide range of people: some who are using only one volume (and doing so alone), others who belong to a community group that plans to discuss each volume, and still others who will organize small community discussion groups. This Guide does not tell you how to read or what to conclude from your reading. It is designed to amplify and complement this particular book.

Section one of this Guide provides questions that may be useful for you to think about while reading the materials and afterward. Questions that are especially appropriate for beginning and focusing discussions are marked with an asterisk (*).

Section two lists phone numbers of organizations and institutions you can call for answers to brief questions about the Soviet Union and U.S.-Soviet relations.

Sections three and four offer guidance for people who want to follow up their reading of these materials by either participating in a discussion group (section three) or undertaking some other type of educational project (section four). The section on discussion groups outlines how they work (from defining the purpose of such groups to wrapping up a meeting), identifies some common problems, and offers a set of models for structuring and running discussion groups. Although the educational projects described in section four can be undertaken by members of a discussion group, they are also activities that individuals can pursue on their own.

The Guide concludes with a short annotated reading list of books and articles.

> **"It is better to know some of the questions than all of the answers."**
> **James Thurber**

I. QUESTIONS

You might want to ponder certain general questions such as the following:

■ What do I think of the Soviet Union? How and why have I formed these impressions?

■ Do I know any Russians or other Soviets?

■ What movies, books, or newscasts can I recall that depict the U.S.S.R. or the Soviet people? How were they portrayed?

■ What is the earliest historical event involving the U.S.S.R. or Russia that I can remember from personal experience? The earliest event I can remember from reading stories and books?

As you read, reflect upon, or discuss each section of this book, you might focus on some of the following more specific questions. (As noted above, questions followed by an asterisk may be especially useful in focusing group discussions.)

Political History

■ What historical and cultural forces motivate Soviet internal and international behavior? American behavior?*

■ What specific (and possibly different) historical events have had a significant influence on Soviet and American perceptions? In what ways?

■ What do we perceive today as most threatening about the U.S.S.R. — its Communist ideology or military power?

■ Are Soviet and American reactions to each nation's attempts to influence the domestic policies of the other similar or different?

■ As Americans, do we accept as credible the historical forces that motivate Soviet behavior?

News Media

■ If Soviet and American media cover the same news events and portray them differently, how does this affect Soviet and American thinking about what happens in the world?*

■ Can one compare the media in the U.S.S.R. to the U.S. media, or is this like comparing apples and oranges?

■ Do Soviets perceive a controlled press as good and a free press as bad?

■ Why do we believe either the Soviet or the American press explanations of the so-called spy dust incident?

■ Do our perceptions of the U.S.S.R. change when new reporters go to Moscow?

Textbooks and Literature

■ What would be the possible results of an American student's using translated Soviet books and a Soviet student's using translated American books?*

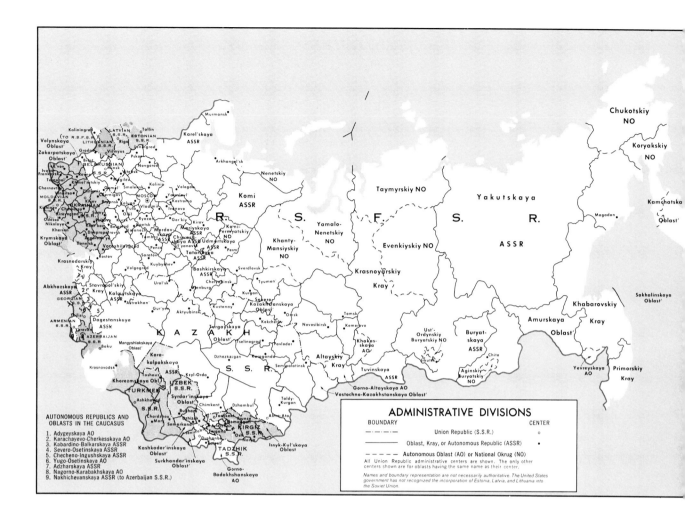

ADMINISTRATIVE DIVISIONS

BOUNDARY	CENTER
‒ · ‒ · ‒ Union Republic (S.S.R.)	○
‒‒‒‒ Oblast, Kray, or Autonomous Republic (ASSR)	•
‒ ‒ ‒ ‒ Autonomous Oblast (AO) or National Okrug (NO)	

All Union Republic administrative centers are shown. The only other centers shown are for oblasts having the same name as their center.

Names and boundary representation are not necessarily authoritative. The United States government has not recognized the incorporation of Estonia, Latvia, and Lithuania into the Soviet Union.

AUTONOMOUS REPUBLICS AND
OBLASTS IN THE CAUCASUS

1. Adygeyskaya AO
2. Karachayevo-Cherkesskaya AO
3. Kabardino-Balkarskaya ASSR
4. Severo-Osetinskaya ASSR
5. Checheno-Ingushskaya ASSR
6. Yugo-Osetinskaya AO
7. Adzharskaya ASSR
8. Nagorno-Karabakhskaya AO
9. Nakhichevanskaya ASSR (to Azerbaijan S.S.R.)

■ Should history textbooks try to avoid reflecting prevailing national political perspectives?

■ Is there a "right" and a "wrong" portrayal of history, or is all history subjective?

■ Do Soviet and American textbooks ignore positive aspects of each nation for similar or different reasons?

■ What would it be like, as is common in the Soviet Union, to seek out and read an officially banned book?

Movies

■ How should we, as an open society, respond to recent complaints about what the Soviets view as offensive, anti-Soviet, American-made movies?*

■ If the American stereotype of Soviets is captured in the (imaginary) movie title "Boy Meets Tractor," what is a movie title that would best reflect Soviet stereotypes of Americans?

■ How would we react to advance publicity for a Soviet movie depicting

U.S. map of U.S.S.R.

Courtesy of U.S. government.

a U.S. invasion of Eastern Europe?

■ If Americans see VCRs as a challenge to Soviet control of information, how are Soviets likely to see the influence of VCRs on American life?

Conclusion

■ Have my perceptions of either the U.S.S.R. or the U.S. been altered by reading *The Other Side*?

■ How relevant are citizen perceptions for U.S.-Soviet relations?

■ Do I now have a more informed view of the Soviet Union?

■ How important are the influences of books, the media, and movies on U.S. and Soviet perceptions of each other?

II. TELEPHONE REFERENCE SOURCES

The telephone permits access to a vast range of information. The following organizations or their libraries may be able to provide you with answers to short questions on the Soviet Union or U.S.-Soviet relations.

American Sources

- Access: (202) 328–2323
- American Association for the Advancement of Slavic Studies: (415) 723–9668
- Committee for National Security: (202) 745–2450
- Department of State, Office of Soviet Affairs: (202) 647–3738
- Harriman Institute for Advanced Study of the Soviet Union, Columbia University: (212) 280–4623
- Institute for Soviet American Relations: (202) 387–3034
- Kennan Institute for Advanced Russian Studies, Smithsonian Institution Libraries: (202) 287–3105
- Library of Congress, Telephone Reference Service: (202) 287–6500
- New York Public Library, Telephone Reference Service: (212) 340–0847; Slavic and Soviet Collection: (212) 930–0714
- Russian and East European Center, University of Illinois: (217) 333–6012

  Your local library may also have a telephone reference service.

Soviet Sources

- Embassy of the Union of Soviet Socialist Republics (hours: 9–12, 3–4:30): (202) 332–1466
- Consulate General of the Union of Soviet Socialist Republics: (415) 922–6642

"Mr. Watson, come here, I want you."
Alexander Graham Bell (speaking the first words transmitted via telephone).

III. EDUCATIONAL PROJECTS

A. Discussion Groups

To continue educating yourself and to begin educating others about the Soviet Union, consider joining an existing community group that might set aside time for interested people to discuss this book. If you are not interested in a discussion group, you might consult the list of other educational projects in part B of this section; it begins on page 149.

Whether you are a participant in a group or someone organizing or leading a discussion group, it is important to remember that such groups can be used and structured in many different ways. There is not a clearly right or wrong method. Various organizations in your community may run discussion groups in different ways. For example, the local World Affairs Council might run monthly discussion groups as a follow-up for a regular program of presentations at a local high school. A local church or temple may have a smaller and more informal group without a regular speaker. The places where groups meet can also vary widely. In addition to schools and meeting halls, local businesses might provide a conference room and refreshments for regular morning or evening discussion groups.

If you cannot find a local group with which you feel comfortable, you might consider starting a discussion group consisting of people you regularly spend time with anyway. If you commute to work with the same group of people every day, why not turn the 30- or 90-minute ride into a discussion of materials from the *Beyond the Kremlin*? A monthly or weekly luncheon dedicated to discussing the series might also suit some people's schedules.

The actual structure of discussion groups is also quite flexible. Some groups may meet only once; others will have a series of meetings. Each person can read his or her copy of the entire book, or teams can be responsible for presenting a summary of particular parts of the volume to the larger group. Visitors might be invited to speak to certain groups at every meeting, every other meeting, or only at the first and last meeting.

The following nine suggestions and questions may be useful to consider regardless of the structure of your particular group and even if you are already a member of an established group.

1. *Focus:*
Without an articulated focus, discussions tend to wander and people can be left frustrated and confused. When possible, the focus for each future meeting should be discussed and determined at the end of the preceding meeting. Each member of the group, particularly new individuals, should have a clear understanding of the basic issue or question to be discussed. In addition, factual materials from the book should be discussed and summarized at the outset of the meeting. This is particularly important because at any particular meeting some members may not

> "Don't let schooling interfere with your education."
> **Mark Twain**

have had time to prepare fully.

The asterisked (*) questions at the beginning of this Guide can be used to help focus a discussion. The following section, entitled "Questions and Answers," illustrates the range of answers that may be offered by members of a discussion group.

2. *Questions and Answers:*
A wide range of views may be voiced in response to discussion questions. The sample below refers to a single question, the first in the news media section: "If Soviet and American media cover the same news events and portray them differently, how does this affect Soviet and American thinking about what happens in the world?

■ "The effect of the media is enormous; look at the differing coverage of the KAL and spy dust stories."
■ "There is no single reality; what the Soviets hear and see reported by the news media is as real to them as what our media reports."
■ "Soviet and American views of what really happened regarding a specific event cannot be so simply compared; the Soviet media intentionally and predictably lies. The Soviets are not even attempting to present reality or the facts."
■ "Media coverage in both countries reflects existing perceptions; the media does not generate new perceptions, it only reinforces old ones."
■ "The American media is as manipulated as the Soviet media, simply by different forces and for different reasons."
■ "The American media generally gives an accurate portrayal of reality; the Soviets also see this same reality, but they distort it."
■ "There is no practical difference between reality and perceptions; if we believe in our perceptions, and what the media tells us, then this is our reality."

Not all these sample answers respond directly to the question posed. This is to be expected. Individual members of a group will interpret questions differently. Although a freewheeling discussion may be helpful initially to encourage open discussion, each member of the group should be aware of the need to maintain a focus — to help bring the discussion back to the specific question being discussed. One way to refocus a confusing discussion might be to rephrase the discussion question. For example: "Leaving aside for the moment which nation's media causes distortions, and which stories are "right" or "wrong," can we agree that Soviet and American citizens perceive events differently? If so, what are the practical implications of this for our government's efforts to deal effectively with the Soviet government?"

3. *Leadership:*
Decide at your first meeting whether the group wants a designated discussion leader. Groups that have operated without leaders when talking about other issues or books might want to consider having one for

this book. Determine the discussion leader's responsibilities (for instance, guiding the discussion, arranging meeting times, and posing and answering questions).

After a leader is selected, he or she should plan to go through this Guide carefully and to prepare for each meeting by elaborating on the points made here. Try to anticipate the discussion by mentally "walking through" the entire meeting before it actually takes place. What questions are likely to be asked? What conflicts might occur? How will the meeting end? What issues are likely to be interesting but frustrating or distracting?

4. *Goal:*

Is the group primarily educational or social in its purpose? Are the group meetings designed to complement or lead into some other type of activity?

5. *Meeting Specifics and Atmosphere:*
■ Where should meetings be held?
■ If one of the aims of the group is to involve new people in discussions of U.S.-Soviet relations, how will they be notified of the group's meetings — by a phone network or announcements in the local paper?
■ Should food be served — drinks, snacks, a meal?
■ How many people should be in the group — 5–10 or 15–25 people?
■ Should the group meet for 45 minutes, 2 hours, or some other amount of time? Should it meet weekly, biweekly, or monthly?
■ Should the group be made up of politically like-minded people, or is a diverse group preferable?

6. *Wrap-Up:*

Determining how to bring meetings to a satisfactory close is difficult. An agreed upon time limit eases this problem but someone still needs to summarize the discussion, noting agreements, disagreements, and unresolved questions. One person might be selected at the start of each meeting to have responsibility for wrap-up.

Discussions aimed at understanding how and why Soviets and Americans view each other in certain ways are likely to provoke further questions and curiosity about many aspects of the Soviet Union. Expect that questions, rather than hard-and-fast conclusions, will result from discussion group meetings. (Some of these questions might be answered by undertaking some of the educational projects suggested in part B.)

7. *Potential Problems:*

As with any collection of people, especially an informal group, successful group relations are very important but difficult to ensure. You should probably anticipate the following:
■ *Attrition:* Throughout the weeks or months that the group meets, people will periodically drop out.
■ *Scheduling:* Most people already have full calendars; becoming ac-

customed to new obligations takes time and committment.

■ *"Hot spots"*: Certain aspects of the Soviet Union and U.S.-Soviet relations are particularly explosive; these will inevitably arise and need to be dealt with. It helps to be aware of some of them and to think about why they are so sensitive. This is especially true if any members of your group have recently traveled to the Soviet Union or emigrated to America. Each member of a group will probably have his or her sensitive issues that may be raised during discussions. Some of these may prompt discussion about the following "hot spots":

■ Dubious political allegiances of peace activists.
■ Abhorrent Soviet treatment of dissidents and religious/ethnic minorities.
■ Self-defeating restrictions on trade with the Soviet Union.
■ Futility of just talking about perceptions and the hopelessness of trying to improve U.S.-Soviet relations.
■ Why certain Soviet aggression is understandable or justified.
■ Obvious similarities between U.S. and U.S.S.R. military activities.
■ Blind distrust for any and everything Soviet.

The "hot spots" just cited were intentionally phrased in a provocative manner, in judgmental and emotional language. Potentially tense situations can often be defused by choosing words that show respect even if they are critical. Topics such as these should not be avoided; they do need to be discussed and will almost certainly arise at some point during the group's meetings. Handling such discussions may be difficult, however, and will tax the diplomatic skills of experienced discussion leaders. A few tips may be helpful:

■ Don't cut people off; let them say in their own words what they feel.
■ Admit to disagreements when they occur; aim for tolerance and understanding of diverse views, not consensus.
■ Acknowledge people's fears and doubts; seek to understand, not dispel, them.
■ Encourage people not simply to restate their views but to share with the group why they hold certain views.
■ Invite group members to respond to all views; if they disagree, encourage them to describe an alternative.

8. *"Why am I doing this?"*:
There will probably come a time when each member of a group will grapple with this question. It is not an easy one, and it generally requires a reassessment of goals — either individuals' or the group's. Groups and members change over time. Some groups may move in directions that alienate certain members. Certain members may undergo experiences that alter their interest or ability to participate. After a few meetings, group time should probably be set aside to discuss both the structure and direction of future discussions, and what has been accomplished so far.

9. *The pontificator vs. the silent one:*
As the saying goes, "there is one in every crowd." Unless your group is chosen quite selectively, there are bound to be members with varied (and sometimes conflicting) styles, mannerisms, and attitudes. If there is one rule that applies to members of small community groups as well as to negotiators for the superpowers, it is that dealing with people who are different from ourselves is difficult but worthwhile. Patience, tolerance, and sensitivity to the needs and fears of others is essential to meaningful discussions.

The final part of this section of the Guide provides three models for how discussion groups might be organized and planned.

Model 1: Complementing Ongoing Activities

Organizers	Community organizations, civic groups, clubs
Frequency	Monthly, first Monday, 7:30 p.m.
Pace and responsibility	Each member reads each chapter, 1 a month
Focus	Topic addressed by guest speaker — summarized at outset of reading
Leadership	Chairperson, sponsoring group
Goal	Education and outreach
Size/location	25–30, classroom
Potential problems	Poor speaker
Wrap-up	2-hour firm limit for meeting

Model 2: Increasing Awareness Among Friends

Organizers	Groups of commuters, neighbors
Frequency	Weekly, Wednesday, 8:15 a.m.
Format	During morning commute
Pace and responsibility	Teams describe chapters to group, 2 meetings per chapter
Focus	Asterisked questions from Reader's Guide
Leadership	Organizer
Goal	Educational use of spare time
Size/location	6 per bus, car, or train
Potential problems	Lack of time, distractions
Wrap-up	Arrival at destination

Model 3: Acquiring In-Depth Knowledge of the U.S.S.R.

Organizers	Travel groups, adult education classes, and others
Frequency	Weekly, during month prior to trip
Format	Pot-luck dinner
Pace and responsibility	Each member reads each chapter, 1 chapter a week
Focus	Questions chosen by group members at planning meeting
Leadership	No single leader
Goal	Preparation for trip
Size/location	8–10, neighbors; apartments or houses
Potential problems	Lack of a leader
Wrap-up	By designated person at each meeting

B. Additional Projects

1. Develop a "Discerning Eye" project to examine and analyze the media, to help yourself and others become more aware of how local media coverage of the Soviet Union influences your community's perceptions of the U.S.S.R.

2. Compare the annotated reading list at the end of this Guide to the card catalog of books available in local public and school libraries. Make suggestions for new purchases or give missing books as gifts.

3. Familiarize yourself with how the U.S.S.R. is portrayed in schoolbooks used in your community.

4. Present contemporary movies, old movies, or slide shows from recent visits to the U.S.S.R. (You may wish to refer to *A Guide to Films About the Soviet Union*, published by the Committee for National Security.)

5. Suggest pairs of movies to be shown (in libraries, theatres, schools, on cable and public television stations) that would illustrate the differing (or possibly similar) ways in which Soviet and American films present issues or stories.

6. Contact the Committee for National Security and indicate your willingness to either give the *Beyond the Kremlin* series to a local library or school as a gift, or to help with the distribution of the series in your community.

7. Offer to provide speakers on the Soviet Union to groups of friends, neighbors, colleagues, or classes.

8. Distribute *Beyond the Kremlin* to readers and organize a regular discussion group (see the earlier section on discussion groups).

9. Plan a local, regional, or national conference on U.S.-Soviet relations (see *Organizing a Conference on National Security*, published by the Committee for National Security).

10. Review or critique this book and other publications on the Soviet Union for a local newspaper, newsletter, or nonprofit organization.

11. Develop a short, informal quiz about the U.S.S.R. and American perceptions of that nation. For example, copy this page and ask people to match the names of the world leader with each statement below. Make sure to include the answers, which can be read by turning this page upside down.

Nikita Khrushchev

Jimmy Carter

Richard M. Nixon

Leonid I. Brezhnev

John F. Kennedy

(Adapted from *Psychology Today* [November 1984] for the Committee for National Security's series *Beyond the Kremlin*. For additional information, please contact the Committee for National Security, 1601 Connecticut Ave. NW, Suite 301, Washington, DC 20009.)

a. "The potential aggressor should know: A crushing retaliatory strike will inevitably be in for him. Our might and vigilance will cool, I think, the hot heads of some imperialist politicians."

b. "We do not want a war. We do not now expect a war. This generation . . . has already had enough — more than enough — of war and hate and oppression. We shall be prepared if others wish it. We shall be alert and try to stop it."

c. "The first use of atomic weapons might very well quickly lead to a rapid and uncontrolled escalation in the use of even more powerful weapons with possibly a worldwide holocaust resulting."

d. "We do not want war. Nor, on the other hand, do we fear it. If war should be forced upon us, we shall know how to rebuff the aggressors in the most decisive fashion. Of this the aggressors are fully aware."

e. "Potential enemies must know that we will respond to whatever degree is required to protect our interests. They must also know that they will only worsen their situation by escalating the level of violence."

f. "The first time one of those things is fired in anger, everything is lost. The warring nations would never be able to put matters back together."

[*Answers:* (a) Brezhnev, (b) Kennedy, (c) Carter, (d) Khrushchev, (e) Nixon, and (f) Brezhnev.]

IV. ANNOTATED BIBLIOGRAPHY

Political History

Filene, Peter, *American Views of Soviet Russia, 1917–1965* (Homewood, Illinois: Dorsey Press, 1968), 401 pages. An excellent collection of speeches, essays, and documents on America's varying views of the U.S.S.R.

Medvedev, Roy, *Let History Judge* (New York: Vintage, 1971), 566 pages. Medvedev, a Marxist historian living in Moscow, analyzes the purges and "the origins and consequences of Stalinism."

Paterson, Thomas (ed.), *The Origins of the Cold War* (Lexington, Massachusetts: D.C. Heath, 1974) 260 pages. An excellent collection of brief essays on the cold war from scholars and statespersons of the day.

Shipler, David, *Russia: Broken Idols, Solemn Dreams* (New York: Times Books 1983), 390 pages. Shipler, a former *New York Times* Moscow correspondent, looks into the feelings and psychology of Soviets in the late 1970s and early 1980s in this excellent book.

Smith, Hedrick, *The Russians* (New York: Ballantine Books, 1976), 682 pages. Written by a former *New York Times* Moscow correspondent, this bestseller offers a fascinating and entertaining look at Soviet life during the heyday of detente.

Talbott, Strobe (ed.), *Khrushchev Remembers* (Boston: Little, Brown, 1970), 618 pages. The memoirs of Soviet leader Nikita Khrushchev and a rare, fascinating, and readable glimpse into the inner circles of Soviet power.

Vaillant, Janet, and Richards, John, *From Russia to U.S.S.R.* (Wellesley Hills, Massachusetts: Independent School Press, 1985), 362 pages. A diverse and interesting collection of documents and narratives on Russia and the Soviet Union.

Wilson, Edmund, *A Window on Russia* (New York: Farrar, Straus, 1972), 280 pages. A collection of insightful essays written over several decades.

News Media

Anderson, Raymond, "U.S.S.R.: How Lenin's Guidelines Shape the News," in *Columbia Journalism Review* (September–October 1984), pp. 40–43. A lively look at contemporary news coverage in the Soviet Union.

Kalb, Marvin, and Rachlin, Samuel, "Cameras and Microphones in Moscow" and "Focus on Moscow," *Nieman Reports* (Cambridge, Spring 1985), pp. 9–14. An American and a Dane discuss their experiences as television correspondents in Moscow.

Mickiewicz, Ellen, *Media and the Russian Public* (New York: Praeger, 1981), p. 156. The best current work on the place of newspapers, television, movies, and the theater in the Soviet Union.

"Books are the treasured wealth of the world."
Henry David Thoreau

Mickiewicz, Ellen, "Soviet and American Television: A Comparison of News Coverage," *Nieman Reports* (Cambridge, Winter 1985), pp. 7–11. A surprising look at the differences and similarities between Soviet and American television.

Powell, Stewart, "The War of Words," *U.S. News and World Report* (October 7, 1985), pp. 34–42. A lively article about the "propaganda wars" between the two superpowers.

Remington, Thomas, "Politics and Professionalism in Soviet Journalism," *Slavic Review* (Fall 1985), pp. 489–503. An interesting look at the training and careers of Soviet journalists.

Schwartz, Morton, *Soviet Perceptions of the United States* (Los Angeles: University of California Press, 1978), 169 pages. The pro-detente views of the U.S.S.R.'s Institute of the U.S.A. and Canada.

Textbooks and Literature

Aitmatov, Chingiz, *The Day Lasts More than a Hundred Years* (Bloomington, Indiana: Indiana University Press, 1983), 352 pages. First published in Moscow in 1980, this remarkable novel blends the space-age future with the Moslem traditions of Central Asia in subtle criticism of Soviet-Russian domination.

Aksyonov, Vassily, *The Burn* (New York: Vintage, 1985), 528 pages. Aksyonov's acclaimed novel captures the rebellious, experimental spirit of Moscow's intelligentsia during the 1960s.

Aksyonov, Vassily, *The Island of Crimea* (New York: Vintage, 1983), 369 pages. A comic and incisive look at modern Soviet life and its relation to the West.

American Association for the Advancement of Slavic Studies, U.S.S.R. Ministry of Education et al., *U.S.-U.S.S.R. Textbook Study Project, Interim Report* (U.S.S.R. and U.S.A.: AAASS, U.S.S.R. Ministry of Education et al., 1981). American educators critique Soviet schoolbooks, and their Soviet counterparts critique American schoolbooks.

Brooks, Jeffery, *When Russia Learned to Read* (Princeton, New Jersey: Princeton University Press, 1985), 356 pages. An interesting study of "literacy and popular literature" in pre-Revolutionary Russia — that is, what ordinary Russians were reading.

Brown, Edward, *Russian Literature since the Revolution* (Cambridge, Massachusetts: Harvard University Press, 1982), 391 pages. The classic work on Soviet literature.

Dovlatov, Sergei, *The Compromise* (New York: Knopf, 1983), 148 pages. A comic yet poignant account of a Soviet journalist's encounters with an oppressive system.

Lyons, Graham (ed.), *The Russian Version of the Second World War* (New York: Facts on File, 1976), 138 pages. The history of World II as taught to Soviet schoolchildren, translated from various Soviet text-books.

Mehnert, Klaus, *The Russians and Their Favorite Books* (Stanford, California: Hoover Institution Press, 1983), 257 pages. A remarkably thorough study of the books that are written and read in today's Soviet Union.

Rasputin, Valentin, *Farewell to Matyora* (New York: Macmillan, 1979), 227 pages. First published in the Soviet Union, this novel chronicles the dangers of reckless industrial development through the destruction of traditional life in the Siberian village of Matyora.

A Soviet View of the American Past (Madison, Wisconsin: State Historical Society of Wisconsin, Madison, 1960), 64 pages. An annotated translation from the section on American history in the *Great Soviet Encyclopedia*.

Voinovich, Vladimir, *The Life and Extraordinary Adventures of Private Ivan Chonkin* (New York: Farrar, Straus, 1977), 316 pages. A hilarious series of misunderstandings follow a simple peasant in Stalin's Red Army.

Voinovich, Vladimir, *Pretender to the Throne* (New York: Farrar, Straus, 1981) 358 pages. The bizarre adventures of Private Chonkin continue in this satire of life under Stalin.

Voinovich, Vladimir, *The Ivankiad* (New York: Farrar, Straus, 1977), 132 pages. A short novel about one writer's battle with the Party bureaucracy.

Movies

Corinth Films (New York: Corinth Films, annual). A diverse catalog of movies available for sale or rental, including many Soviet classics and contemporary films.

Leyda, Jay, *Kino: A History of the Russian Film* (New York: Collier Books, 1973), 465 pages. A thorough study of Russian and Soviet film since 1896.

Marshall, Herbert, *Masters of the Soviet Cinema* (Boston: Routledge and Kegan Paul, 1983), 230 pages. This book focuses on the giants of Soviet cinema such as Sergei Eisenstein.

Mickiewicz, Ellen, *Media and the Russian Public* (New York: Praeger, 1981). The best current work on the place of newspapers, television, movies, and the theater in the Soviet Union.

"U.S.S.R.," *International Film Guide.* Published annually, this yearbook on international films includes a fine chapter on the Soviet Union that surveys the overall state of the Soviet cinema and also reviews individual movies.

General

Cohen, Stephen, *Sovieticus: American Perceptions and Soviet Realities* (New York: Norton, 1985), 154 pages. An insightful collection of brief essays from a liberal perspective.

Hough, Jerry and Fainsod, Merle, *How the Soviet Union Is Governed* (Cambridge, Massachusetts: Harvard University Press, 1979), 576 pages. Professor Hough's revision of Fainsod's classic *How Russia Is Ruled.*

Medish, Vadim, *The Soviet Union* (Englewood Cliffs, New Jersey: Prentice-Hall, 1984), 344 pages. A good basic text on the U.S.S.R., which includes many useful facts, figures, and other information.

Pipes, Richard, *Survival Is Not Enough* (New York: Simon and Schuster, 1984), 281 pages. U.S.-Soviet relations from a conservative viewpoint.

Pond, Elizabeth, "Shades of Communism," *The Christian Science Monitor,* (January 7, 1986), pp. 17–19. An insightful long article about the Soviet Union after seven decades of Communist rule and the prospects for its future.

Schmemann, Serge, "The View from Russia," *The New York Times Magazine* (November 10, 1985), pp. 51–64. An excellent article by a Moscow correspondent examining the sources of Soviet perceptions of the U.S.

Sivachev, Nikolai, and Yakovlev, Nikolai, *Russia and the United States* (Chicago: University of Chicago Press, 1979), 269 pages. Two Soviet authors describe U.S.-Soviet relations from their viewpoint.

V. BEYOND THE KREMLIN

Topics to be addressed in future *Beyond The Kremlin* volumes may include:

Women in the Soviet Union

Defense and the Soviet military

Ideology, religion, and values

Negotiating with the Soviets

U.S.S.R. and the world economy

Soviet foreign policy

Soviet government

Diversity in Soviet society

Daily life

Youth in the Soviet Union

The Soviet future